ABOUT THE AUTHOR

Killian H. Gore was born in Fort Phantom in Texas in 1976. He is a distant relative of the serial killer Ellen Mort who was born in Liverpool, England and later vanished in Salt Lake City, Utah, after violently butchering all five of her husbands (*for the full true story of Ellen Mort, read my Incredible Horror Movie Facts book*).

He is the author of the short story collections *Before Halloween* and *Three Tales of Terror* as well as the novellas *Beyond Bigfoot*, *The Thingy From Another World* and *The Demon of Heritage* - and also the serialized horror story, *The Horror Movie Massacre*.

His short films *Schrecken*, *Two Ghost Tent* and *Don't Look at the Camera!* appear in the *60 Seconds to Die* horror film series. He is also an Associate Producer of the 2020 summer camp slasher movie, *Bloody Summer Camp*, starring Felissa Rose.

His hugely entertaining *What's Your Favorite Scary Movie?* book features interviews with such horror legends as Joe Dante, Michael Berryman, Richard Stanley, John A. Russo, Marcus Nispel, Fred Dekker, William Malone and Mark Shostrom. He's also written a whole bunch of quiz books! Listen out for Killian on *The Huge Horror Movie Podcast* on YouTube.

He lives in Warrington, England.

www.facebook.com/killianhgore
www.twitter.com/killianhgore
www.instagram/killianhgore
For SIGNED COPIES check out the
Killian Gore Store on Etsy

Also by Killian H. Gore

Before Halloween
The Thingy From Another World
Beyond Bigfoot
The Demon of Heritage
Three Tales of Terror
The Horror Movie Massacre: Book One

Non-fiction:

The Unauthorized Friday the 13th Quiz Book
The 'Burbs Unauthorized Quiz Book
Incredible Horror Movie Facts
The Evil Dead Unauthorized Quiz Book
What's Your Favorite Scary Movie?
Phantasm Unauthorized Quiz Book
The Thing Unauthorized Quiz Book
Jaws Unauthorized Quiz Book
The Monster Squad Unauthorized Quiz Book
The Shining Unauthorized Quiz Book
The Huge Horror Movie Quiz Book
Gremlins Unauthorized Quiz Book
Plan 9 from Outer Space Quiz Book
Horror Movie Crossword Book
Halloween Unauthorized Quiz Book
The Mini Horror Quiz Collection Series

Collections:

Gore-Lore: The Collected Works of Killian H. Gore
Horror Quiz Book Collection
Horror Quiz Book Collection Part II
Joe Dante Double Bill Quiz Book
Mini Horror Quiz Collection 1-4 and 5-8

THE HORROR MOVIE MANUAL

An A-Z of Everything You Did and Didn't Know

By
Killian H. Gore

CONTENTS

<u>Foreword</u>

First of all, if you already have a copy of my book, *The Horror Movie Dictionary* (and you probably don't, because that's why I've created this new edition!), then please ask for a refund. *The Horror Movie Manual* is basically the same book. I've added a few new entries and got rid of a couple of things, but that's about all. Why did I decide to do this? Well, if you were to ask me what I regard as my best book, I would say it's this one. But, for whatever reason, it never seemed to find an audience. At all! So, I wanted to do what the old B-movie horror filmmakers used to do. If a movie tanked at the box office, they would change the title and produce a new poster and give the film another try. And that's all I'm doing here. I want to give my work another go, because I think it deserves it.

And if it doesn't work, please expect another release this time next year of *The Horror Movie Guidebook*.

My very best wishes,

Killian
February 2020, Warrington, England

A

Abby - The name of a female vampire that you probably shouldn't let in.

Afraid - Something we should be whilst watching horror movies. And *very* afraid if it's *The Fly* (1986).

AIDS (Astro Investigation and Defense service) - A New Zealand-based organization that was sent to the village of Kaihoro to thwart the plans of an invading alien race intent on harvesting humans for fast food. Features in *Bad Taste* (1987).

Airplane Wing - A place where nervous passengers are most likely to view a hideous gremlin-like creature trying to sabotage the plane's engines.

Alien - A creature from another planet. Aliens take many forms in horror movies from gelatinous blobs to shapeshifting entities, ravenous tooth-heavy beasts, humanoids, robots, enormous monsters, tiny parasites or the more traditional large-eyed little green men (aka Greys). Whatever they appear like, they want to kill us all. Notable alien horror movies: *The Blob* (1958/1988), The *Alien* movies (1979-2017), the *Predator* movies (1987-2018), *The Thing* (1982), *Monsters* (2010), *Attack the Block* (2011) and *Slither* (2006).

Alien Abduction - Sometimes alien beings want to take humans up onto their flashy spaceships, but not to show-off about how much better their technology is, rather to perform intrusive experiments on us and generally frighten us. Notable movies include *Communion* (1989), *Fire in the Sky* (1993), *The Fourth Kind* (2009) and *Dark Skies* (2013).

Alucard - Dear lord, no! It's Dracula spelled backwards!

Amazon Rainforest - The world's largest rainforest and home to countless tribes of hostile and violent cannibals - sometimes referred to as the Green Inferno. Notable horror films set in the Amazon rainforest include: *Cannibal Holocaust* (1980), *Cannibal Ferox* (1981),

White Slave aka *Amazonia: The Catherine Miles Story* (1985) and *The Green Inferno* (2013).

Amity Island - The name of the fictional island featured in the *Jaws* movies. It's supposed to mean "friendship", but that bothersome great white shark swimming around in the waters is anything but friendly.

Amityville - A village located in the town of Babylon, Suffolk County in New York. In a large Dutch Colonial house in Amityville at 112 Ocean Avenue, Ronald DeFeo Jr. murdered six members of his family in 1974. The following year, the Lutz family moved into the house and stayed for 28 days. They weren't very keen on ghosts. Author Jay Anson wrote a book about their stay in the house, which was turned into a movie, which spawned over three thousand sequels. Okay, so it wasn't quite that many (it just feels like it). At the time of writing there are around twenty *Amityville* movies.

Ancient Ones - A monstrous group of giant creatures that live under the Earth and require the blood from a bunch of cliché horror movie characters in order to save all of us from being devoured by them. Features in *The Cabin in the Woods* (2012).

Anger - An emotion experienced by many horror movie fans when another remake is announced (although they often end up liking the movie).

Annabelle - The name of the creepy doll that is the central antagonist in *The Conjuring* movies and spin-offs. Annabelle is based upon a real, allegedly demonically possessed Raggedy Ann doll, also named Annabelle. It was committed to a glass cabinet by Ed and Lorraine Warren at their occult museum in Connecticut, adorned with the warning "Positively do not open." Naturally, with a warning like that, everybody who visits probably opens it when no one's looking.

Ant - A ubiquitous insect with antennas on their heads that live in colonies run by a queen ant. Even though they're impressively strong for their size, they're generally a bit of a nuisance and get all over everything - some of the little bastards even have wings! They can usually be found crawling over rotten food or dead creatures in horror films. Sometimes they take a more central focus as the main antagonists. Notable horror movies include: *Them!* (1954), *Phase IV* (1974) and *Empire of the Ants* (1977).

Anthology Horror Films - A style of horror film consisting of a selection of shorter horror movies, usually with different stories, locations and characters, though often narratively tied together with a wraparound story, or a particular theme. Notable examples include *Creepshow* (1982), *Dead of Night* (1945), *Twilight Zone: The Movie* (1983), *Tales from the Crypt* (1972), *Trilogy of Terror* (1975) and *Trick 'r Treat* (2007)… and, okay, my *60 Seconds to Die* movies.

Antichrist - Someone who is an opponent of Christ and intends to rule over the world until Christ's second coming. In horror movies the antichrist is often portrayed as the son of Satan, namely in *The Omen* and *Rosemary's Baby*, but the Book of Revelation does not specifically state this.

Antonio Bay - A fictional location in California. Probably not the best place to visit if it's foggy. Features in *The Fog* (1980).

Anubis - The name of an ancient Egyptian god who judges the dead, featuring in the 2014 film *The Pyramid*. The incredibly ugly Anubis (who, to be fair, is over 3000 years old) has a grisly habit of removing people's hearts whilst they are still alive to determine if they are worthy to enter the afterlife or not. Of course, the problem with this method of judgement is that the person being judged ends up dead anyway.

Apocalypse Trilogy - The name given by director John Carpenter to refer to his three, bleak-world-view movies: *The Thing* (1982), *Prince of Darkness* (1987) and *In the Mouth of Madness* (1994).

Arawak (Camp) - The name of the summer camp featured in the slasher movie *Sleepaway Camp* (1983). According to the poster, you won't be coming home from it – a good option if you wish to cut down on travel expenses.

Area 51 - A top secret government facility that will all know about, which is filled with crashed flying saucers and aliens. Features prominently in the 2015 found-footage horror movie *Area 51*.

Arrow Video - A specialist distribution label created by Arrow Films to release classic, cult and obscure horror movies, often with brand-new restorations and a wealth of bonus features.

Arrow - A sharp, thin implement that is shot from a bow, usually by Robin Hood. It also comes in handy as a method to kill folk in horror movies. Saw Tooth in the *Wrong Turn* movies enjoys twanging an arrow at people and Jason Voorhees in the *Friday the 13th* movies has also flirted with an arrow or two as a death purveyor.

Art the Clown - A seriously freaky, sadistic and demented clown who appears on Halloween night. Art enjoys creepily watching people, doing the usual comical clown stuff, and violently slaughtering people. Not advisable to book him for a children's party. Art most notably features in the 2016 movie *Terrifier* and was played by actor David Howard Thornton, although he first appeared in the 2013 horror anthology film *All Hallows' Eve*, played by Mike Giannelli.

Ash - A Hyperdyne Systems 120-A/2 android featured in the 1979 movie, *Alien*. Ash wasn't the post popular of crewmembers onboard the Nostromo, which is probably on account of favoring the newly acquired alien lifeform at the expendability of everyone else's lives. Ultimately, they ganged-up on him and knocked his head off - literally.

Asylum - An alternative name for a psychiatric hospital. Asylums are usually completely abandoned in horror movies and contain ghosts. Notable examples: *Session 9* (2001), *Grave Encounters* (2011) and *House on Haunted Hill* (1999).

Audrey Two - A plant from outer space with a bloodlust - it's a surprisingly good singer, though. Audrey II's nickname is Twoey.

Autopsy - The chopping up of a dead body to determine the cause of death – turned out to be a very bad idea when attempted on the body of an anonymous women in *The Autopsy of Jane Doe* (2016).

B

Babadook - If it's in a word or it's in a look, you can't get rid of the Babadook. Now, if you've just read that, you will be relentlessly haunted by a creepy bogeyman who wears a black coat and a black hat and has clawed hands. He originates from a really rather cool-looking children's pop-up book, but don't be deceived by it, for it heralds the arrival of the demonic Babadook, also known as Mister Babadook. Even really annoying children won't scare him away.

Baby Jane - I'm not quite sure what happened to her.

Babysitter - A person (usually female) charged with looking after the children of neglecting parents (whilst they cavort around town enjoying themselves) who are tormented and often killed by an escaped lunatic. Alternatively, it is the babysitters themselves who turn out to be bat-shit-crazy.

Babysitter (and the man upstairs) - An urban legend concerning a babysitter who receives menacing or creepy phone calls, which are revealed to be coming from within the house. Notably features in the films *Black Christmas* (1974) and, more faithfully adapted at the beginning of *When a Stranger Calls* (1979).

Backwards – Don't walk in this direction in a horror movie as you are likely to walk into the bad guy - or a ghost, or monster, so just something terrifying! Alternatively, you'll just walk into one of the other characters or a cat if it's a false jump-scare.

Bad Movie - Perhaps more so than in any other film genre, "bad" horror movies are often celebrated by horror fans. Also referred to as, "So bad, they're good," the movies tend to exhibit poor scripting, direction, acting, special effects and production values, but rather than disregard them, certain movies have endured and gained cult followings and loyal fans over the years. Intentionally attempting to create a "bad" horror movie is something of a futile task as perhaps one of the most likeable attributes is the sincerity of the production - in other words, the movies are entertaining because the filmmakers genuinely believed they were making a good movie. Notable examples include *Plan 9 from Outer Space* (1959), *Silent Night, Deadly Night 2* (1987), *Troll 2* (1990) and *Birdemic: Shock and Terror* (2010).

Bagul (or Bughuul) - The name of an ancient, demonic, Babylonian deity who collects the souls of children. On account of having no mouth, Bagul is rather quiet and "his thing" is to force children to murder their families in terribly gruesome ways and have them film the event – the idea being that images of Bagul can aid the demon to enter the mortal world from the spirit world. He appears in the 2012 film *Sinister* and its 2015 sequel. Despite his fun-sounding alternative name of Mr. Boogie, he's not really much of a dancer.

Baker, Angela - The killer in the *Sleepaway Camp* movies. Angela was born as a boy, named Peter, who lost his sister, also named Angela, in a boating accident when he was a young child. It was as a result of this that Peter was forced to take on the identity of his deceased sister by her strange Aunt Martha. After a murder-filled, fun-packed trip to Camp Arawak, Angela showed her penis to everyone (with her mouth agape in a peculiar and terrifying manner). Some years later, Angela returned to camp, this time as a camp counselor at Camp Rolling Hills (in *Sleepaway Camp II: Unhappy Campers*) where she killed another bunch of people. And not intent on having killed all those people, she went to Camp New Horizons (in *Sleepaway Camp III: Teenage Wasteland*) and Camp Manabe (*Return to Sleepaway Camp*) to kill some more. She is portrayed in parts 1 and 4 by Felissa Rose and Pamela Springsteen in 2 and 3.

Balloon - A flexible bag that is inflated and floats. They all float down here.

Banana Splits, The – A jovial gang of musical animals from the 1960s portrayed by actors inside some pretty wacky costumes. The consisted of Fleegle, Bingo, Drooper and Snorky and entertained kids with their fun and groovy antics on a popular Hanna-Barbera television show. Much to everyone's surprise they became rather violent in 2019.

Barbra - They're coming to get her.

Barrow - The name of a real small town in Alaska (now known by the far catchier name of Utqiagvik) that was used as the setting for the vampire movie *30 Days of Night* (2007), owing to its extended period of darkness. In reality the town experiences over sixty days with no sunlight. So, they got that wrong, didn't they?

Basement (aka cellar) - A room in a building that is either fully or partially underground. Commonly they house boilers, fuse boxes, air conditioning units and junk that nobody uses but can't bear to part with. In horror movies, all sorts of terrors lurk down there. Notable examples: *The Evil Dead* (1981), *It* (2017), *The Silence of the Lambs* (1991) and *The Conjuring* (2013).

Bates Motel - The establishment owned and run by Norman Bates in *Psycho*, with a little bit of help from his deceased mother. The room rates are pretty good, and the linen is always clean but, things can get a bit "stabby" in the shower.

Bates, Norman - A fictional character from the *Psycho* movies and *Bates Motel* TV show. Norman was the creation of writer Robert Bloch in his 1959 novel, *Psycho*, and was loosely based on the murderer Ed Gein. He was portrayed in the four *Psycho* movies by Anthony Perkins. Norman's hobbies include slightly heated conversations, taxidermy, cross-dressing, murder and disposing of dead bodies.

Bats - A type of flying mammal heavily associated with the horror genre, probably because they scare the bejesus out of most people by noisily flapping around in dark places and drinking blood. Bats are also synonymous with vampires – who have the ability to turn into them. They are ALWAYS in caves in horror films and also around spooky old castles.

BB - The name of the artificial intelligence robot featured in Wes Craven's *Deadly Friend* (1986) who was initially destroyed before having its AI chip implanted into the almost-dead body of a girl named Samantha Pringle. It made her go a bit "kill-happy," shall we say.

Beartrap – A device for trapping bears, which some idiot always goes and steps into whilst running away from danger in a horror movie.

Beast - A dog that has the odd distinction of being one of the only canines in motion picture history to have its own flashback scene. Features in *The Hills Have Eyes Part II* (1984). Director Wes Craven was said to have disowned the movie. It probably has something to do with *that* dog flashback scene.

Beast, The - An alternative name of the main antagonist featured in the *Poltergeist* film series. He also goes by the more friendly name of Reverend Henry Kane.

Beelzebub - An alternative name for the Devil and a word from Queen's *Bohemian Rhapsody*.

Beer - The favorite drink of most teens in slasher movies. Drinking it usually leads to imminent death.

Belial, Bradley - The name of the deformed conjoined twin featured in the three *Basket Case* (1982 – 1991) movies. Since being separated from his much better-looking brother, Duane, Belial was subjected to life in a basket. He is very small, very twisted and very mad… according to the movie poster. But I suppose anyone would be under those circumstances.

Beyond - Something that is far away, or on the other side. It's a popular horror movie title word too. Example horror movie titles: *The Beyond, From Beyond, Beyond Re-Animator and From Beyond the Grave*.

Bigfoot - A hairy, upright-walking creature that enjoys hiding from everyone in the woods of North America. Despite no documented real-life cases of a Bigfoot (also known as Sasquatch) attacking or killing anyone, if you encounter one in a horror movie it is most likely to kill you. Notable examples: *Night of the Demon* (1980), *Abominable* (2006), *Willow Creek* (2013) and *Exists* (2014).

Billy - The name of the freakish puppet featuring in the *Saw* film franchise. Billy's role is to deliver recorded messages (and, obviously to give the people the willies) by John Kramer, the Jigsaw Killer, to explain the deadly situation the victims have just found themselves in.

Billy, Lenz - The mostly unseen killer in the 1974 film *Black Christmas* (and the 2006 remake). He enjoys making very weird prank phone calls… and killing people. It is suggested that the character of Eugene in *Behind the Mask: The Rise of Leslie Vernon* is an elderly version of Billy Lenz.

Bioraptor - An aggressive alien creature, not so keen on light. They prefer it pitch black, actually.

Birds - Winged creatures that flap around peacefully in the sky, not usually bothering humans, aside from the occasional defecation on our unsuspecting heads. However, in 1963 they surprisingly turned on us rather epically in Bodega Bay, California. The incident was caught on camera by Alfred Hitchcock in the imaginatively titled film, *The Birds*.

Bisgetti - Canned spaghetti in tomato sauce that has the ability to turn into worms – but only if a flat-sharing vampire casts a spell over you. Features in *What We Do in the Shadows* (2014).

Blade (Eric Brooks) - A fictional half-vampire, vampire-killer character created by Marv Wolfman and Gene Colan in 1973. Blade, as portrayed by Wesley Snipes in the *Blade* film trilogy (1998-2004), has all the strengths of a vampire, but none of their weaknesses. He's not particularly good at filing his income tax returns, though.

Blade - The name of the lead killer in the *Puppet Master* film franchise. Blade has a skull-like face, a knife for one arm, and a hook for the other; he wears a black trench coat, has white hair and, within the mythology of the *Puppet Master* universe, was created by André Toulon using the soul (well, brain-tissue) of a German scientist named Dr. Hess. Along with the puppets Pinhead and Jester, Blade has appeared in all of the *Puppet Master* movies, of which there are many.

Blair Witch - The titular character from *The Blair Witch Project* (1999). Her real name was Elly Kedward (or more fully, Eilis Abaigeal Kedward) and, though she's only spoken of in the film, there are various descriptions of her given, which range from an old woman dressed in black to a more monstrous creature covered in hair, who floats. The Blair Witch continues to haunt the Black Hills Forest in Burkittsville to this very day.

Blaxploitation Horror - A subgenre of horror films mostly featuring black actors. The word is both derivative of the words "black" and "exploitation," which you'd probably already worked out yourself. Blaxploitation films emerged when oppressed black filmmakers decided they wanted to create films aimed more towards their own culture. They often parodied typical white-created stereotypes of themselves and infused their horror movies with a high sense of comedy and parody. Some of the most notable blaxploitation horror movies include *Blacula* (1972), *Blackenstein* (1973), *Abby* (1974), *Sugar Hill* (1974) and *Dr. Black, Mr. Hyde* (1976).

Blob, The - A gelatinous and monstrous alien being (1958), or a gelatinous and monstrous military experiment (1988), depending on which film you're watching. The Blob gets larger the more people it consumes. Its main weakness is ice – so it would have been a rather short film if it had appeared at Outpost #31. Bizarrely there is some basis in reality for *The Blob* as in 1950 four police officers in Philadelphia reported seeing a saucer-shaped object glide down to Earth. When they approached the craft, they witnessed it was a glowing purple blob. Although it didn't eat everybody and grow larger, it just evaporated after around twenty minutes – which wouldn't have made such an entertaining movie, really.

Blood - The red liquid circulating throughout human and vertebrate animal's bodies. In horror films, it's usually not in the body where it's supposed to be. It's usually all over the place.

B-movie - A low budget film that used to be shown before the main feature in movie theaters. The term now refers to any particularly schlocky film. In the 1950s, horror became a popular genre for B-movies with legendary filmmaker Roger Corman being at the forefront of low-budget, quickly shot horror flicks, earning him the nickname "King of the Bs." Sometimes, when a B-movie failed at the box office, the producers would change the title and create a new poster and put the movie out again. Rather like what I did with this book.

Bob, Killer - An interdimensional entity who possesses people in the town of Twin Peaks. Styled as Killer BOB. Features in the movie *Twin Peaks: Fire Walk with Me* (1992).

Body Count - Usually synonymous with the slasher movie sub-genre, 'body count' (or kill-count) refers to the amount of people killed during the movie. It is common for sequels to increase the body count. The theatrical poster for *Friday the 13th Part 2* (1981) features the tagline, "The Body Count Continues…" Strangely there are actually less deaths in part 2, though.

Body Horror - A subgenre of horror movie in which particularly gruesome and gory things happen to the human body. Canadian filmmaker David Cronenberg is often cited as the originator of the subgenre with films such as *Shivers* (1975) and *Rabid* (1977).

Body Snatcher - *See "Pod People".*

Bogeyman - A scary, imaginary character used to frighten children into behaving themselves. There are a wide variety of bogeyman legends all over the world, all serving the same purpose. In Haddonfield, Illinois, in the late seventies, the bogeyman, as a matter of fact, became real.

Bones - Separate parts of the skeleton inside a human or animal body. Ignited dog urine can have the capability to reconfigure human bones back into their skeleton form and infuse them with fresh flesh to resurrect nightmarish bogeymen. But this only happened once.

Boogie, Mr. - *See "Bagul."*

Book of the Dead - *See "Necronomicon."*

Boomstick - The nickname given by Ash Williams for his twelve-gauge double-barreled shotgun. Although the gun appears in the first two *Evil Dead* movies, Ash doesn't refer to it as a "boomstick" until the third movie, *Army of Darkness*.

Boreham Caverns - A chartered cave system completely devoid of subterranean, predatory creatures. It would have been a less lively choice for the characters in *The Descent*, but a pretty dull movie.

Brains - Something the living dead like to snack on.

Breather, The - The nickname of the killer in the 1981 slasher film parody, *Student Bodies*. The Breather wears garden gloves and kills people in rather silly ways, whilst breathing heavily, obviously. One of his more absurd murders involves killing a lady with paperclips.

Brewster, Charley - The main protagonist in *Fright Night* (1985). He's *so* cool.

Bride, The - The name given to the female counterpart of Frankenstein's monster. The Bride's most famous screen incarnation is in the 1935 film *Bride of Frankenstein* in which she was portrayed by Elsa Lanchester with the now iconic conical hairdo with white lightning streaks on each side.

Brides of Dracula - The collective term for the three groupie female vampires who often hang around Count Dracula in adaptations of the Bram Stoker novel.

Brightburn (Brandon Breyer) – A superhero with a similar backstory to Superman who thought it would be more fun to use his superpowers to creep everybody out with… and kill the people. Brightburn is also the name of the Kansas town in which Brightburn crash-lands. Which is a remarkable coincidence.

Bruce - The nickname given to the mechanical shark(s) in Steven Spielberg's 1975 film, *Jaws*. Bruce famously was an immensely awkward giant puppet that mostly wouldn't behave in the way the filmmakers wanted it to and was largely responsible for the film going overbudget and off-schedule. Bruce was named after Spielberg's lawyer, Bruce Ramer. The crew had taken to a far more derogative moniker and called it, "The Great White Turd". "Bruce the Rubber Shark" was actually given a Worst Career Achievement Award at the Golden Raspberry Awards in 1987.

Brundlefly - The name given to the hybrid of Seth Brundle and a housefly after they successfully made it through a teleportation machine together. In retrospect, Seth wished he'd gone through alone.

Bub - The name of the zombie featured in *Day of the Dead* who is trained to be a bit less "bitey" by the character Dr. Logan.

Bubba Ho-Tep – An ancient Egyptian mummy who dresses like a cowboy and lives in a retirement home. He's eventually set on fire by Elvis Presley with some help from John F. Kennedy. You had to be there.

Bubblegum - A type of chewing gum that can be blown into a bubble. If you run out of it, the best alternative is to kick ass.

Bucket - A watertight container for holding liquids. In horror movies it's usually filled with blood. Used in a horror film title: *A Bucket of Blood (1959)*.

Buddi – A brand of high-tech, interactive doll that everyone initially wanted to hate when they first heard about it. And then we found out Mark Hamill was doing the voice and we changed our minds.

Burlap sack - Also known as a gunny sack, gunny shoe or tow sack – a cheap bag traditionally made from hessian. Initially *Friday the 13th*'s bogeyman, Jason Voorhees, wore a burlap sack over his head, but the movie merchandising people stepped in and suggested people weren't all that likely to buy an official movie-tie-in burlap sack to go trick or treating in, rather they'd just buy a cheap one from the supermarket, so they changed it to a hockey mask for *Friday the 13th Part III* (1982). Burlap sacks can also be seen in the horror movies *The Town That Dreaded Sundown* (1976) and the 2014 sequel of the same name, *Dark Night of the Scarecrow* (1981), *The Orphanage* (2007), *The Strangers* (2008), *Triangle* (2009) and *Trick 'r Treat* (2007).

Busan - A large port city in South Korea. But, be warned - the train ride there may be riddled with the undead. Features in *Train to Busan* (2016).

Butterball - The obese and incredibly ugly, shades-wearing, cenobite featured in the first two *Hellraiser* movies, played both times by actor Simon Bamford. Before his life got rather hellish, Butterball was a glutenous sinner named Laslo who relentlessly sought pleasure, to the point of being attracted to a shiny little puzzle box that brought him a rather abnormal version of pleasure that he wasn't quite expecting.

Bye Bye Man - A demonic bogeyman who stalks and kills anyone who says or even thinks of his name. Oops. I just thought of it. And so did you.

C

Cabin - A small house usually made of wood and, more often than not, located miles from anywhere, deep in the woods. Bad things tend to happen in and around them. Notable appearances include *The Evil Dead* (1981), *Cabin Fever* (2002), *Tucker and Dale vs Evil* (2010) and *The Cabin in the Woods* (2011).

Cabin Fever - The term used to describe the madness a person can succumb to if stuck indoors in an isolated location for a long period of time (especially with Shelley Duvall). Jack Torrance in *The Shining* experienced it and went completely batshit crazy.

Cadaver - The name given to a dead human body. The word is more frequently used to refer to a dead body being used by medical students to study. Cadavers can provide lots of gratuitous gore in horror films as well as providing some frights when they twitch… or come back to life.

Cady, Max - The name of a violent ex-convict who lawyers should really think twice about representing. Cady went and made himself book-smart whilst in jail and relentlessly pursued his lawyer all the way to Cape Fear, where he tried to spoil his family vacation.

Caligari, Dr. - The name of the crazy hypnotist in the influential German Expressionist movie *The Cabinet of Dr. Caligari* (1920). Caligari uses a sleepwalking man named Cesare to commit murders for him, but in a twist that M. Night Shyamalan wished he'd thought up, the whole thing turns out to just be in the mind of a mental asylum inmate.

Calvin - The name of the alien creature from the film *Life* (2017). Calvin was named by a bunch of schoolchildren from Calvin Coolidge Elementary School (clearly, they put a lot of thought into that). Not content with wiping out all life on Mars, Calvin, via the International Space Station, moved to Earth where he's currently waiting for the greenlight for a sequel to kill everyone there too.

Camp Blood - A nickname for Camp Crystal Lake from the *Friday the 13th* movies. Presumably the name derives from the fact that it's a camp where lots of blood has been shed.

Camp Crystal Lake - The name of the summer camp in the *Friday the 13th* film franchise. Despite being synonymous with the franchise, Camp Crystal Lake doesn't centrally feature in many of the movies as an active summer camp - in fact, it has only been the case in one of the movies: *Friday the 13th Part VI: Jason Lives*, although it was renamed Camp Forest Green (the rebranding was to disassociate itself from the murders that had taken place there in the past – although maybe *not* opening any new summer camps in the area would have been a more sensible idea). The original *Friday the 13th* was filmed at a real summer camp in New Jersey called Camp No-Be-Be-Sco. To this day it remains an active summer camp and is proud to have had no actual murders take place there, so far.

Campfire - A controlled fire that people gather around in the wilderness (or at summer camps) to burn marshmallows and tell scary stories. If there's a campfire story being told in a horror movie, then it's more than likely going to come true and everyone's going to get killed. Notable appearances include *The Fog* (1980), *Friday the 13th Part 2* (1981), *Madman* (1981) and *Sleepaway Camp II: Unhappy Campers* (1988).

Camp Rolling Hills - The name of the summer camp featured in *Sleepaway Camp II: Unhappy Campers*. Keep your distance from the camp counselor named Angela.

Camp Stonewater - The name of the summer camp featured in the 1980 slasher movie *The Burning*. Jason Alexander from *Seinfeld* was in attendance, alongside the Oscar winning actress Holly Hunter. Neither of them really enjoyed their time there as they were bothered by a badly burned "camp legend" named Cropsy who rather enjoyed butchering campers with a pair of gardening shears.

Candyman (Daniel Robitaille) - The name given to the man originally named Daniel Robitaille who was cruelly tortured and murdered before returning as a hooked-hand killer whenever someone uttered the name "Candyman" in the mirror five times. His name derives from the method in which he was killed (stung to death by bees) and he's considered to be an urban legend around the Cabrini-Green housing project in Chicago. Unfortunately for an eager, young graduate student, named Helen Lyle, it turns out he's real. Candyman has been portrayed in the three movies, *Candyman*, *Candyman: Farewell to the Flesh* and *Candyman: Day of the Dead*, by actor Tony Todd.

Cannibal - A person who eats the flesh of another person. Cannibals were predominately found in the jungle in the seventies and eighties run of Italian cannibal films, but have also branched out into other subgenres, such as the slasher movie (*Wrong Turn*), serial killer movie (*The Silence of the Lambs*) and musical comedy horror film (*Cannibal! The Musical*).

Cannibal films - A subgenre of horror film that was at its most popular in the seventies and eighties and was usually made by Italian filmmakers. Typically, the films were set in third-world jungles and featured scenes of torture, rape, real footage of animal cruelty and, of course, cannibalism (although, weirdly, not always). The 1972 film, *Man from Deep River*, is usually cited as the first cannibal film, although it is Ruggero Deodato's 1980 film *Cannibal Holocaust* that is generally viewed as the most famous and notorious.

Canuxploitation - A term referring to the spate of horror (and other genre) movies made in Canada between 1974 and 1982, when a tax-shelter, introduced by the Canadian government to boost film production, made shooting films in Canada a much cheaper option for filmmakers. Notable films from the era include *Black Christmas* (1974), *Shivers* (1975), *Happy Birthday to Me* (1981), *Prom Night* (1980) and *Visiting Hours* (1982).

Carmilla - The name of a female vampire and an 1872 novella by Joseph Sheridan Le Fanu, predating the more famous *Dracula* novel of 1897. Carmilla is viewed as the source for horror films featuring lesbian vampires. Hammer's 1970 film *The Vampire Lovers*, starring Ingrid Pitt, is based upon the story.

Castle Rock - The name of a fictional town featured in many Stephen King books and film adaptations. Not an ideal place to live.

Cell-phone - A battery-operated device for making wireless telephone calls. In horror movies they are commonly used by killers to freak out their potential victims. They also have an odd habit of not working at most horror film locations.

Cenobite - An extradimensional being from the *Hellraiser* film series. They are partial to wearing S&M-style clothing and adore torturing and mutilating anyone who pays them a visit after successfully solving the Lament Configuration puzzle box. Their leader is a very welcoming demon known as Pinhead who, appearances aside, says such warm and friendly things as, "We have such sights to show you!" before spoiling everything and declaring, "We'll tear your soul apart!"

Chainsaw - A portable mechanical saw commonly used for tree felling. In Texas its predominate use is to dismember out-of-towners.

Changeling - A child secretly exchanged by the parents for another child. The 1980 movie, *The Changeling*, featured a storyline, supposedly based on a real-life incident, in which such a substitution occurred. It didn't end well.

Chatterer - A rather toothsome and gruesome Cenobite from the *Hellraiser* movies. Despite the prominence of his mouth and teeth, he doesn't say an awful lot. He pretty much just clicks his teeth together.

Cherry Falls - A small American town in Virginia where it is actually *unsafe* to be a virgin in a slasher movie, for a change.

Chess Wizard - A computerized chess game in which the human opponent plays against the machine. If the human opponent feels like they are losing the game, it is recommended that they pour whiskey into the computer.

Chianti - A wine produced in the Chianti region of Tuscany, Italy. Goes very well with fava beans and census takers.

Chopper - Something one should run to with a sense of urgency.

Chop-Top (Sawyer) - A deranged, sadistic killer from Texas who also likes to scratch around the metal plate on his head with a clothes hanger that he heats up with a lighter, before munching on the cooked flesh. Hey, don't knock it till you've tried it! He is portrayed by horror movie stalwart Bill Moseley in *The Texas Chainsaw Massacre 2* (1986).

Christine - The name of a possessed Plymouth Fury car featured in John Carpenter's 1983 film adaptation of Stephen King's novel, *Christine*. The car, owned by Arnie Cunningham, is possessed, indestructible and enjoys killing people. He did get it at a very good price, though.

ChromeSkull (Jesse Cromeans) – A psychopathic serial killer and amateur filmmaker who wears, you've guessed it, a chrome skull mask. As he can't talk ChromeSkull uses audio samples of his victims' final moments to communicate with others. I'd like to see him try to order a Happy Meal.

Chucky - The name serial killer Charles Lee Ray became known as when he transferred his soul into a doll. Chucky, like his former human incarnation, is a malevolent character who kills people in a wide variety of horrific and creative ways. He's absolutely hilarious though, so that makes it all okay. He has appeared in seven *Child's Play* feature films so far, every time voiced by actor Brad Dourif (who also appears in some of the films as the human version of Chucky).

Chud (or C.H.U.D.) - An acronym for Cannibalistic Humanoid Underground Dweller. Chuds are human-like cannibals who live below the surface. I don't think I actually needed to explain that, though. Sorry.

Chum - A bloody liquid consisting of fish parts, bones and blood that is put into the ocean in order to attract sharks… who then eat you.

Church - The name of the cat in *Pet Sematary* (1989). Church got really pissed after he was killed on a busy road and then buried in a malfunctioning ancient Indian burial ground. And then he got killed again. On the bright side… seven more lives to go!

Clover (Cloverfield Monster) - The name given to the giant monster featured in *Cloverfield* (2008). Despite some debate over its origin, with some suggesting it's extraterrestrial, the filmmakers have stated that it is an amphibious organism. In *The Cloverfield Paradox* (2018) it is shown to have possibly originated from another dimension. Wherever it came from, and whatever it is, it's a mean and nasty creature hellbent on destruction. And it hates the Statue of Liberty.

Cleaver - A large, heavy knife used for chopping people up with.

Clown - A comical performer who wears exaggerated makeup and clothing. They're usually found in the circus and are supposed to be funny, but the horror genre decided otherwise and thought they were far better suited to being scary. Quite possibly this began when it was discovered that the lovely Pogo the Clown was revealed to be the notorious serial killer John Wayne Gacy. Notable horror movie clowns include: Pennywise, Art and the Killer Klowns from Outer Space.

Coffin - A wooden box in which humans (and sometimes animals) are buried in. Vampires use them to sleep in, because they're a bit weird, and zombies break out of them because they get a ravenous craving for human flesh.

Collector, The – The alias of a sadistic killer and insect fan. The Collector, whose real name we don't know, excelled in killing entire families – leaving one of them alive (aww, that's nice) who he would add to his collection, but would also kill and arrange their body parts and bones to resemble insects (oh… not so nice).

Colonial Theatre - The name of the movie theater in Phoenixville, Pennsylvania, USA, which featured in the 1958 classic horror movie, *The Blob*, during the iconic sequence in which everybody runs screaming from the theater when the creature oozes through the projection room windows into the audience. There is a commemorative plaque inside the Colonial, near to the projection room, that reads, "Through this wall in the year 1958 Shorty Yeaworth's THE BLOB brought the monster into the movie theater and Phoenixville's COLONIAL THEATRE into the annals of film history.

Comedy horror - A subgenre of horror movie in which a few laughs are thrown in amongst the scares. Not to be confused with certain so-bad-they're good horror movies, which are unintentionally funny.

Conjuring Universe - A contemporary group of successful American horror movies connected (sometimes rather loosely) by the cases of the real-life paranormal investigators Ed and Lorraine Warren. The series began in 2013 with *The Conjuring* and most recently a third *Annabelle* spinoff (*Annabelle Comes Home*) and *The Curse of La Llorona* (2019) have been released. A proposed third *The Conjuring* movie is set for a release in 2020. To date, the 2018 spinoff *The Nun* has been the most financially successfully, though, conflictingly, the most critically panned. Thus, conclusively proving, once and for all, that critics are stupid.

Cornfield - Normally a patch of land where corn is grown, though in Nebraska they are also home to a malevolent entity known as "He Who Walks Behind the Rows." And he sure does a hell of a lot of walking having featured in ten movies to date, all (aside from the first one and the TV remake) incredibly loosely based on Stephen King's short story, *Children of the Corn*.

Coven - A bunch of witches, gathered together to cast their wicked spells. It is sometimes considered to be a group of thirteen witches - but however many witches you can pull together at short notice will do.

Cranberry sauce - A fruity relish made from cranberries, typically served with turkey at Thanksgiving or Christmas. It most definitely is *not* the red substance featured in *Blood Rage* (1987).

Crawlers - A human-like species that frequent uncharted cave systems in the Appalachian Mountains. *The Descent* director, Neil Marshall, describes them as, "Caveman that never left the caves." Crawlers are blind but have a very keen sense of hearing - so, best not to set any alarms on your watch. They enjoy climbing, killing, eating and unexpectedly popping up in the background of camcorder shots.

Creep, the - A skeletal storyteller featured in the *Creepshow* movies. He doesn't say an awful lot (nothing at all in the first movie), which is a bit strange for a storyteller. The animatronic puppet used whilst making the first movie was nicknamed Raoul by the special effects crew.

Creeper, the - The name of the rather mysterious, ancient demon featured in the *Jeepers Creepers* film series (2001-2017). Unlike most other movie monsters, The Creeper is rather limited to only being able to hunt for 23 days, every 23rd spring – so he makes sure he makes the most of it during that time. The Creeper has been portrayed in all three *Jeepers Creepers* movies to date by the same actor - Jonathan Breck.

Creepshow - A fictional horror comic book based on the comics released by EC Comics and featuring in the *Creepshow* horror films. Contains particularly gruesome horror tales, presided over by a character known as The Creep.

Creepypasta - Horror stories or images with an urban legend vibe that have been copied and pasted on the Internet. The word is derived from "copypasta," which is a slang term for copying and pasting text. Perhaps the most well-known Creepypasta is the legend of the Slender Man.

Cricket bat - A particularly effective weapon in the case of a zombie apocalypse. Features in *Shaun of the Dead* (2004).

Crites - The name given to the alien species featured in the *Critters* film franchise (1986-1992). Crites are hedgehog-like in appearance, although they differ quite considerably from their terrestrial lookalikes. For instance, they have multiple rows of very sharp teeth, red eyes, the ability to shoot out poisonous barbs and they like to kill and eat people. They'll pretty much eat whatever is in their path and sometimes that path is much larger if they choose to join together to form a large Crite ball. They're pretty hard to totally eradicate as they appear to breed like rabbits.

Crocodile - A large aquatic reptile that eats humans. Crocodiles and alligators are just as monstrous in real-life and their kind has been around since the time of the dinosaurs. They kill around 1000 people per year. Crocodiles glide silently through the water, with the top part of their bodies (sneakily) resembling water before bursting out when you get too close, dragging you under for a bit of death-roll fun, then taking you back to a more private location to eat you. In horror films they can often be portrayed by poorly rendered computer-generated imagery in a slew of direct-to-video titles such as *Croc* (2007), *Supergator*

(2007) and the *Lake Placid* films (from part 2 onwards). Notable good crocodile movies include: *Death Trap* (1976), *Lake Placid* (1999), *Rogue* (2007), *Black Water* (2007) and *Alligator* (1980).

Cropsy - The name of the killer in the 1981 slasher movie *The Burning*. Cropsy was badly burned during a summer camp prank that went terribly wrong and, not seeing the funny side, returned to slaughter everyone – at a completely different camp! Perhaps his eyesight wasn't too good after the accident. He is based upon the actual New York urban legend of Cropsey; a campfire tale of a bogeyman who abducts and kills campers. Cropsy is still apparently out there right now, so it's best to not look, breathe, or move, or you'll end up dead.

Cross - An object resembling a crucifix that is used to cause harm to vampires. It can be made from a variety of materials, including twigs, pencils, popsicle sticks, or even fingers (although that's not usually terribly effective).

Crossover horror films - A not particularly widespread type of horror movie that features characters from different film franchises. The height of its popularity was arguably with the Universal Monster movies, in particular the spate of *Abbott and Costello Meet...* movies in the 40s and 50s. Horror crossovers did score some success in more recent times with the movies *Freddy vs. Jason* (2003) and *AVP: Alien vs. Predator* (2004), but most of the time they are reduced to direct-to-video fare such as *Puppet Master vs Demonic Toys* (2004), *Gingerdead Man Vs. Evil Bong* (2013) and the ridiculously titled *Lake Placid vs Anaconda* (2015).

Crowley, Victor - The main antagonist of the *Hatchet* (2006-2017) film franchise who resides in Honey Island Swamp. He was accidentally struck in the face by his own father with a hatchet on Halloween night after some local bullies set fire to his house. It wasn't a good day really. Years later he returned as a vengeful spirit to brutally kill anyone who trespassed on his land. Despite his signature weapon being a hatchet, Victor's most entertaining on-screen killings often involve him simply using his hands to rip people to pieces. He is portrayed in all four of the *Hatchet* movies by iconic horror actor Kane Hodder.

Crucifix - Either a wooden cross used for crucifying people or an ornamental sculpture depicting Christ on the cross. It comes in handy for warding off evil or for freaking out vampires – but, don't bother using one on the vampires featured in *Interview with the Vampire*, as they, weirdly, quite like crucifixes. Occasionally it has far more disturbing uses (*The Exorcist*).

Cryptkeeper - The name of the storytelling, wisecracking skeletal host featured in the *Tales from the Crypt* TV show and movie spin-offs (*Demon Knight, Bordello of Blood* and (kind of) *Ritual*). The Cryptkeeper has a seriously demented sense of humor, heightened by his witch-like evil laugh. He was voiced by actor John Kassir and his on-screen appearance was achieved by the use of an elaborate puppet.

Cryptozoology - The branch of science, not taken particularly seriously by scientists, that relates to the study of all the monsters that we really wish were real. Some of the best-known cryptids include Bigfoot, The Loch Ness Monster, Chupacabra and the Jersey Devil. I've seen them all… in horror movies, that is.

Crystal Lake - The central location in the *Friday the 13th* film franchise situated in Wessex County. Primarily it seemed like it was merely the name of the lake and the summer camp (Camp Crystal Lake), but over the course of the franchise it became known as the name of the town too.

Cthulhu - The name of the monster created by H. P. Lovecraft in his short story *The Call of Cthulhu*, described himself as, "A monster of vaguely anthropoid outline, but with an octopus-like head whose face was a mass of feelers, a scaly, rubbery-looking body, prodigious claws on hind and fore feet, and long, narrow wings behind." Pretty freaky, then.

Cube, The – A giant and mysterious cube full of booby-traps in which strangers awaken to find themselves having to think really hard about mathematics or they get killed. I'd be totally screwed.

Curse - A spoken spell-like, supernatural utterance to bring bad luck or harm to someone. Once a person becomes successfully cursed, it's usually pretty difficult to break that curse. The character of Christine Brown in *Drag me to Hell* (2009) had a curse put on her by a creepy-looking old lady (who got a bit uppity when she was refused a time-extension on her loan) and tried everything (even killing her own cat!) to get rid of it. Nothing worked and she currently resides in Hell.

Objects can also be cursed and dispel bad happenings on the person or persons who unwisely choose to meddle with the particular cursed item.

Cursed films - Supposedly certain horror movie productions and/or sets or locations have had curses on them – usually movies connected with the occult or supernatural. Notable examples include *The Exorcist* (the set burned down, and actor Jack McGowran died shortly after filming), *The Omen* (a car crash involving a decapitation - next to a road sign for Ommen: 6.66 km) and *Poltergeist* (actress Dominique Dunne killed by her boyfriend and Carol Anne actress, Heather O'Rourke, dying at just 12-years-old).

Cujo - A St. Bernard dog who was bitten by a rabid bat, which literally sent him bat-shit crazy and hellbent on attacking Dee Wallace and her young son. Features in the 1983 horror movie, *Cujo*, based on Stephen King's 1981 novel of the same name.

Cypher, Louis - The name of the character played by Robert De Niro in the 1987 film *Angel Heart*. Louis Cypher… say it fast… Lucifer. He's the Devil!

D

Damballa chant - A chant (that can be found in *Voodoo for Dummies*) that features in the *Child's Play* movies and has the power to transfer souls. Used in a quote: "Abe due Damballa. Give me the power, I beg of you!" Damballa is actually a god who is the creator of life in Haitan Vodou (Voodoo).

Dandrige, Jerry - An apple-munching vampire who is likely to overstay his welcome if invited into your house by your rather naïve and smitten mother.

Darkness - A word for either a location devoid of light or a term used to describe evil, for example *Prince of Darkness*. Horror movies feature both uses of darkness rather predominately.

Dark Universe - The name given to the proposed new cinematic universe based on the classic Universal Monsters. Universal made a couple of attempts at starting this universe, first with *Dracula Untold* in 2014 and then with *The Mummy* in 2017. Neither effort seemed to take hold, and Universal announced in January 2019 that it was abandoning the concept of interconnecting the movies and would, instead, create more standalone movies such as Leigh Whannell's (*Saw, Insidious*) *The Invisible Man* (2020).

Darkman (Peyton Westlake) - The central character featured in the three *Darkman* movies: *Darkman* (1990), *Darkman II: The Return of Durant* (1995) and *Darkman III: Die Darkman Die* (1996). Despite his gloomy-sounding name, Darkman is basically a good guy, despite once shouting at his girlfriend on a pleasant trip the funfair to, "Take the f**king elephant!".

Dates, your - The good news is, they're here! Unfortunately, they're dead. Sorry about that.

Dawn - The time of day when the sun is just beginning to rise. The dead also tend to rise around that time too. The word can be found in a number of horror movie titles (because it sounds a little spooky). Some examples include: *Dawn of the Dead* (1978/2004), *From Dusk Till Dawn* (1996), *Just Before Dawn* (1981) and *Dead Before Dawn 3D* (2012) – also *Evil Dead II*'s subtitle – *Dead by Dawn*.

Day - A commonly used horror movie title word. Some examples include *Day of the Dead* (1985), *The Day of the Triffids* (1962), *Graduation Day* (1981), *Candyman 3: Day of the Dead* (1999) and *April Fool's Day* (1986).

Daywalker - A vampire who's not really all that bothered about sunlight.

Dead - The state of being dead, which sometimes it's better to be in - especially if the alternative is being buried in a faulty Indian burial ground. Dead is also a very ubiquitous word in horror movie titles. Some examples include: *The Evil Dead* (1981), *Night of the Living Dead* (1968), *Freddy's Dead: The Final Nightmare* (1991), *City of the Living Dead* (1980), *Dead Snow* (2009) and *Dead Silence* (2007).

Deadite - In the *Evil Dead* movies and TV show, a deadtite is anything that has become possessed by a Kandarian Demon. Pretty much anything can become a deadtite (including desk lamps) but more often than not, it's a person. Deadites tend to have white eyes, demonic features, a very threatening manner, enhanced strength and durability, regenerative powers and a penchant for comedic violence. Decapitation is highly recommended to thwart them but attacking them with a Kandarian Dagger (if you can get hold of one) is the best method to stop them.

Deadly Spawn - Freaky aliens from outer space with lots and lots of teeth. Absolutely loads of them, in fact.

Death - Although you could argue that death is actually the villain in most horror movies, as a character Death is more literally the main antagonist featured (but not seen) in the *Final Destination* movie series. This is on account of the characters in the franchise always cheating death at the start of each film by avoiding an accident that someone has a premonition about. An angered Death then seeks out those people and makes them have an incredibly gruesome but thoroughly entertaining death.

Deaths-head (hawkmoth) - The type of moth featured on both the theatrical poster for *The Silence of the Lambs* (1991) and also as a prominent part of the film's narrative. The deaths-head moth gets its name from what appears to be a natural skull design on its back — saving themselves a trip to the tattoo parlor.

Decker, Dr. (Philip K. Decker aka Button Face) – A masked serial killer who turned out to be horror film director David Cronenberg! We should have known. Features in Clive Barker's *Nightbreed* (1990.)

Demon - An evil spirit whose favorite movie genre is horror. Demons, in their various guises, are frequently referenced and featured in horror movies.

Demonic Possession - A form of spiritual possession by a demonic entity. Seldom do good spirits seem to possess anybody in horror films. People who have become possessed tend to act very bizarrely, sometimes speaking in languages they aren't familiar with and contorting their body in physically challenging or impossible ways. In real life, people claiming to be demonically possessed are probably just a bit mad, but in horror films it tends to be a genuine malevolent demon who has a hold on them. A good-ole exorcism usually calms the symptoms, and a good night's rest.

Demonic Toys - Having already ripped-off *Child's Play* with the *Puppet Master* films, producer Charles Band opted to rip-off his own movie and create the Demonic Toys. Despite just being a bunch of (albeit creepy-looking) toys, the Demonic Toys are actually demons from hell! Their leader is Baby Oopsy Daisy, who swears a lot and kills people with whatever weapon is to hand. The other members of the gang are Jack Attack, Grizzly Teddy, Mr. Static, Zombietoid and Divoletto. They're a lot like the *Toy Story* characters, except they like to murder people.

Depladon (aka Euypterid Monster) – A large (and seriously ugly) sea monster encountered by the crew of the DeepStar Six Naval facility. There's a lesson to be learned here. If you find an underwater cave system, don't blow it up to see what's inside. You probably won't like what you find.

Derry – A picturesque town in Maine. Just stay clear of the storm drains.

Dhampir - A creature spawned from a vampire mating with a human.

Dinosaurs - The collective name for a group of extinct reptiles that lived many moons ago. They became extinct 65 million years ago (special thanks to the *Jurassic Park* poster for that particular fact) and owing to their rediscovery, through the fossils that they thoughtfully left behind, they have become a great addition to the world of horror movie monsters. Though not often featuring in too many full-on horror movies, their monstrous appearance and size has seen them become horror stars in the films they feature in, particularly the *Jurassic Park* film series (1993-2018). Along with many other large monsters, dinosaurs have made a fair few appearances in low budget horror films in such titles as *Carnosaur* (1993), *Raptor* (2001), *Triassic World* (2018), *The Jurassic Games*, *KillerSaurus* (2015), *Jurassic Predator* (2018), *The Dinosaur Project* (2012) and Poseidon Rex (2013).

Direct-to-video - A term referring to a movie that doesn't have a theatrical release, often due to being a low-budget production. Though it's not exclusive to the horror genre, direct-to-video titles are quite often low-budget horror films – perhaps as a result of the genre not always having the same box office clout as other more family-orientated genres that appeal to a wider audience.

Djinn, The - Also known as The Wishmaster, The Djinn is the central villain in the *Wishmaster* film series. He's an evil wish-granting genie (rather demonic in natural appearance but able to shapeshift into human form) who gives people three wishes, which he takes rather literally or manages to put a bit of a grisly twist on in order to kill or harm the wish maker. He is played by Andrew Divoff in the first two movies and John Novak in the second two.

Doe, John - The name of the serial killer in the 1995 movie *Se7en*. Joe Doe is also the name used for unidentified dead bodies, or a name used to conceal the identity of someone. Variants include: Jane Doe (for females), John Roe, Richard Roe, and Baby Doe, Janie Doe and Johnny Doe for children.

Dolarhyde, Francis - The real name of the Tooth Fairy. Unfortunately, he's not someone who swaps your baby teeth for money.

Dracula, Count - The name of the titular character in Bram Stoker's 1897 seminal vampire horror novel. Count Dracula is loosely based on Vlad the Impaler and is arguably the most famous vampire creation in history. Despite Dracula's personality charms, he's a cruel and vicious predator who enjoys a good ole drink of fresh blood. He has exceptional strength and can shape-shift into a variety of creepy animals, as well as a mist – basically he's like the Superman of vampires. There have been countless appearances of the character in horror movies, dating back to the early days of cinema although, debatably, his most iconic appearances are Béla Lugosi and Christopher

Lee's portrayal of him.

Dracula's Castle - The home of Count Dracula in Transylvania. In reality there are a few castles which claim to be the real Dracula's Castle (probably so they can all sell vampire and Dracula goodies in the gift shop). Bran Castle markets itself as the real Dracula's Castle, with little evidence to support the claim (they think Vlad the Impaler may have been there once). Other castles include Poenari Castle and Hunyad Castle (aka Corvin Castle). Some scholars believe it is actually the Scottish Slains Castle that inspired Stoker's descriptions of Dracula's Castle.

Dreams – Before Freddy Krueger came along, dreams were thought to be a safe place to be in a horror film. Ah well. We can always dream of the day when... oh, no. No we can't do that.

Dream demons – The creepy little tykes that gave Freddy Krueger the ability to be able to kill people in their dreams.

Driller Killer (Reno Miller) – An artist who will drill into your head with a power drill if you don't like his paintings – or just drill into anyone he meets whether you've seen his paintings or not.

Drive-in theater - An outdoor venue where films are projected onto a movie screen in front of a large area for people to park their cars and view the film from. Despite the first drive-in opening in 1933, they didn't reach their peak in popularity until the late 50s/early 60s. They were the perfect setting to view horror movies as screenings had to take place at nighttime (so people could actually see them), and so they became rather synonymous with the genre. They also feature in a number of horror movies, most notably *Drive In Massacre* (1976), *Chillerama* (2011), *The Monster Squad* (1987) and *Blood Rage* (1987).

Dull boy - The result of all work and no play, especially if you're named Jack.

E

Ectoplasm - A gooey substance that ghosts exude. Dr. Peter Venkman (Bill Murray) got covered in it in *Ghostbusters* (1984), provoking him to utter the memorable line, "He slimed me."

Eden Lake - A lovely, picturesque lake surrounded by woodlands, ideal for a romantic getaway. Try not to let the local kids spoil your weekend, though.

Eel Marsh House - An English manor house near Crythin Gifford located on a small island, which is only accessible when the tide is out — this, together with the hauntings, don't make it a very suitable destination for a weekend getaway. Features in *The Woman in Black* (2012).

Electric chair - An execution device used for sadistic serial killers to initially kill them, before granting them the opportunity to return as an even deadlier version of their former selves. Notable examples include: *Shocker* (1989), *Prison* (1987), *House IV: The Horror Show* (1989) and *Destroyer* (1988).

Elevator - A small, box-like structure for transporting lazy people to higher or lower floors in a building. Maybe on account of an elevator's confined space, or its guillotine-potential sliding doors, they can often feature in horror movies. One of the most iconic elevator appearances is arguably the scene from *The Shining* in which a huge amount of blood inexplicably oozes out from the doors. I've no idea why, it's probably symbolic or something.

Eli - The name of a young girl vampire (who's actually a lot older than she looks) who is quite choosey about letting the right person in on her little secret.

Elm Street - The main stomping-ground of Freddy Krueger in the *A Nightmare on Elm Street* film series. In the first movie the action is centered around 1428 Elm Street, which is the home of the film's protagonist Nancy Thompson. The same house later becomes known as Freddy's house. Whosever house it is, Elm Street is not a safe street to bring your kids up in.

Elvira (Mistress of the Dark) – One of the most iconic horror hostesses and star of two feature films, *Elvira: Mistress of the Dark* and *Elvira's Haunted Hills*. Known for her gothic look, smart mouth and her, erm, haunted hills. Portrayed by actress Cassandra Peterson.

Elvis Presley - An iconic American singer who was thought to have died in the late seventies, although he is currently believed to reside in the Shady Rest Retirement Home in Texas where he fights ancient mummies to pass the time. Features in *Bubba Ho-Tep* (2002).

Emergo - A movie theater screening gimmick involving a skeleton model with illuminated red eyes being swooshed over the audience via wires. Pioneered and applied by filmmaker William Castle during screenings of *House on Haunted Hill* (1959).

Empire International Pictures - An independent film distribution company that specialized in producing and distributing low budget horror and fantasy films, formed by Charles Band in 1983. Some of its more notable horror flicks include *Ghoulies* (1985), *Re-Animator* (1985), *From Beyond* (1986), *Rawhead Rex* (1986), *Troll* (1986), *TerrorVision* (1986), *Creepozoids* (1987) and *Dolls* (1987).

Engineers - A race of ancient extraterrestrials who created human beings (and also wanted to destroy us – which is a bit weird). Engineers are rather human-like, except much taller and paler and hairless and seemingly devoid of a sense of humor (I've never seen one laugh). Like most people, I'm rather fuzzy on their origins and intentions. Feature in *Prometheus* (2012).

Ennis House - A real house in Los Angeles, California that has appeared in countless movies. Its most notable horror appearance is in William Castle's 1959 film, *House on Haunted Hill.*

Event Horizon - The name of the starship featured in the 1997 film of the same name. The Event Horizon was thought to have vanished on its maiden voyage but was rediscovered seven years later, having been to hell and back, literally. The consequences of its trip to the hellish dimension it visited were that the ship itself become demonically possessed. As its creator, Dr. William Weir said, "She tore a hole in our universe, a gateway to another dimension. A dimension of pure chaos. Pure… evil. When she crossed over, she was just a ship but, when she came back, she was alive." A lot of gory deaths ensued.

Evidence bag - A plastic or paper bag used to store items from a crime scene for forensic testing, investigation and criminal prosecution purposes. In horror films the police or detectives, or pretty much just anybody standing around, tend to naively contaminate crucial evidence by picking it up without wearing protective gloves. It's no wonder that prolific killers like Jason Voorhees and Michael Myers tend to evade the authorities with such slippery police work.

Exorcism - The religious practice of dispelling demons from an unwelcoming host (or place). Arguably the most famous horror film exorcism was the rather difficult removal of the demon Pazuzu from Regan MacNeil in *The Exorcist* (1973). The word in context: "What an excellent day for an exorcism."

Exorcist - The title of a person who performs an exorcism. Father Merrin from *The Exorcist* movies is probably the most well-known horror movie exorcist.

Exploitation - The name given to any lower budget movie that capitalizes on other more successful movies. They tend to be filled with excessive sex, violence, gore and everything else we like in a movie.

Extraterrestrial - The name for an alien from another world. Extraterrestrials are rarely friendly creatures in horror movies, with some exceptions.

Eyes - Apparently Michael Myers from the *Halloween* film series possesses the blackest ones. But they are hidden behind a mask most of the time, so that's kind of cheating.

F

Facehugger - The name for a breed of alien that leaps onto your face, usually from out of an oversized egg. Once on your face, the facehugger will plop the embryo of a terrifyingly ugly and deadly Xenomorph into your body that will hatch with a shocking burst of blood from your stomach. It's not advisable to take photos of the birth.

Fake shemp - A term coined by *The Evil Dead* director Sam Raimi to refer to stand-in actors replacing the principal cast for shooting additional scenes. In Raimi's case it was on account of the film's low budget that he was unable to bring back the main cast and so various "Fake Shemps" were used to enable Raimi to finish the movie. In some cases, notably Ed Wood's *Plan 9 from Outer Space* (1959), a Fake Shemp was used because the lead actor had died. The origin of the term comes from the death of *The Three Stooges* actor Shemp Howard, whose premature death during the production of a number of short *Three Stooges* films prompted the use of a stand-in to complete the movies.

Familiar - The name for either a witches' animal assistant or a mortal human who is in service and under the control of a particular vampire. In Bram Stoker's *Dracula*, the character of Renfield is Count Dracula's familiar.

Familicide - The term for a type of murder in which the perpetrator kills his or her family members, before killing themselves. It can also be referred to as Family Annihilation. Notable horror movie example: *The Amityville Horror* (1979).

Fan film - An independently made and unofficial (usually) short horror film using characters, locations and story elements from a well-known and much-loved horror film (and other genre-films too). Certain fan-films have become rather elaborate and even include stars from the original films. Vincente DiSanti's 2017 *Friday the 13th* 54-minute fan-film, *Never Hike Alone* (starring Thom Mathews from *Friday the 13th Part VI: Jason Lives*) is perhaps one of the greatest examples of a successful fan-film. Copyright infringement tends to get overlooked, as long as no profits are made from the films.

Fang - A long and rather sharp tooth that monsters and vampires tend to bite us with.

Fangoria - The name one of the most popular horror movie magazines in the world that was first published in 1979. Fangoria also produce horror films, comic books and are behind the Fangoria Chainsaw Awards, which first began in 1992, to celebrate achievements within horror filmmaking.

Father's Day – A day of celebration in which some fathers whine on and on about having some cake.

Fear - The emotion we experience whilst watching horror movies. Well, ideally anyway.

Filicide - The term used for a parent killing their child. Notable horror movie example: *Mom and Dad* (2017).

Final - A word used rather frequently in horror movie sequel's subtitles to suggest it's the final movie in the franchise - although in the majority of cases another sequel follows. Notable examples include: *Omen III: The Final Conflict* (followed by two more movies); *Freddy's Dead: The Final Nightmare* (followed by three more movies) and *Friday the 13th: The Final Chapter* (followed by eight more movies).

Final boy - The last surviving male character in a slasher horror movie. Not as common as the "Final Girl" but there are a few notable examples – perhaps the most well-known is Jesse in *A Nightmare on Elm Street 2: Freddy's Revenge* and the character of Tommy Jarvis in *Friday the 13th* parts 4 to 6.

Final girl - The last surviving female character in a slasher horror movie. The term was first used in the book *Men, Women, and Chainsaws: Gender in the Modern Horror Film* (1992) by Carol J. Clover. The final girl defeats the killer at the end of the movie, but often gets killed herself if a sequel is made. Sometimes it doesn't even matter if she gets killed in a sequel as she could still come back to kill the murderer again – example: *Halloween* (2018).

Firefly Family - The name of the group of serial killers in Rob Zombie's horror movie trilogy consisting of *House of 1000 Corpses*, *The Devil's Rejects* and *3 from Hell*. The main three members of the family are Captain Spaulding (Sid Haig), Otis Driftwood (Bill Moseley) and Baby Firefly (Sheri Moon Zombie).

Flight 180 - A doomed Boeing 747 flight featured in the *Final Destination* film series. Student Alex Browning had a premonition of it crashing and so disembarked the plane with a small group of other people he'd freaked out. They all thought they were safe until that killjoy, Death, decided otherwise.

Fluffy - A rather benevolent-sounding name for an incredibly malevolent creature (although never actually named in the movie). Fluffy features in the story segment *The Crate* in *Creepshow* (1982), and, according to the writing on the outside of the crate, the creature originates from the Arctic and was obtained on an 1834 expedition. The yeti-like creature has lots of very sharp teeth and enjoys devouring everyone who comes in contact with it.

Folk horror - A horror movie subgenre featuring storylines usually concerning alternative or ancient religions, Paganism, Satanism, ritualistic behavior, nature deities, stone circles, etc. The quintessential folk-horror movie is generally regarded as *The Wicker Man* (1973).

Found Footage - A sub-genre/style of horror movie in which the narrative is presented as if the viewer is being shown "real" footage from a particular event. Ruggero Deodato's 1980 *Cannibal Holocaust* is most often cited as one of the first movies to utilize the technique, although it was the 1999 film *The Blair Witch Project* which redefined and popularized the medium. Once *Blair Witch* proved to be such a box office smash, any old Joe with a video camera pretty much thought they could do the same thing. Despite the oversaturation of the style resulting in over four billion awful horror movies, there continue to be a few that use the technique to brilliant effect. Some great examples include *[Rec]* (2007), *Paranormal Activity* (2007), *Troll Hunter* (2010), *Creep* (2014) and *The Visit* (2015).

Frankenstein - The name of a novel by Mary Shelley, first published in 1818, and also often used as the name of the creature created by

Victor Frankenstein in the story. *Frankenstein* is one of the most popular and well-known horror stories ever written – and incredibly it was written by an eighteen-year-old, for a bet! Unfortunately, these days bets amongst teenagers amount to nothing more than a poorly filmed video on YouTube involving stripping, drinking, or sitting in a bath of iced water. The story of *Frankenstein* basically involves a scientist creating a monster from pieces of dead people, which is reignited with life. The monster, obviously, is a bit of an unstable character and Victor doesn't really want him around the house, so it goes off and kills a few people before eventually ending up killing itself after Victor's death. There have been countless film versions, although the 1931 Universal Studios adaptation remains the most iconic.

Friday - A particularly bad day to be in attendance at a summer camp. Especially if it falls on the 13th of the month.

Frog Brothers - The collective name of Edgar and Alan Frog from *The Lost Boys* films portrayed by Corey Feldman and Jamison Newlander, respectively. As well as running a comic book store in Santa Carla, the Frog Brothers like to scare brightly dressed youngsters about the vampires running rampant in their town. They also enjoy killing them. Their Christian names obviously are derived from Edgar Allan Poe's name.

Full Moon Features - An American film production and distribution company famed for its low budget horror movies, most notably the *Puppet Master* movies, *Subspecies, Trancers, Killjoy* and *Demonic Toy* films. The company, headed by Charles Band, is now called Full Moon Pictures.

Further, The - A rather hellish other dimension inhabited by the dead and malevolent. Features in the *Insidious* movies.

G

Gardening shears - Also known as pruning shears, hedge clippers or secateurs; gardening shears are a scissor-instrument used to clip trees and hedges and sometimes fingers and other body parts in locations where teenagers are present. Notable films: *The Burning* (1980) and *Friday the 13th: A New Beginning* (1985).

Gargoyle - An ugly stone, demonic-like sculpture, often adorned to the exterior of churches to keep evil out and usually with an open-mouth that acts as a waterspout. Gargoyles can often appear in more Gothic-style horror movies, on the side of spooky old building or castles, accompanied by a flash of lighting and a rumble of thunder.

Garlic - A strong-tasting foodstuff that can be useful for determining if someone is a vampire or not or for protecting yourself against a vampire. It doesn't always work, though – the head vampire, Max in *The Lost Boys* likes garlic, but not in large quantities.

Gas mask - A mask that is worn to prevent the wearer from breathing toxic or harmful fumes or gases. Owing to the large eye holes and elongated design of the mouthpiece on certain gas mask models, they are particularly well suited to appearances in horror films. Perhaps the most iconic gas mask-wearing movie villain is Harry Warden (aka The Miner) featured in the classic 1981 slasher movie, *My Bloody Valentine*.

Gatlin - A Nebraskan town where everybody is crazy about corn. The children all prattle on about somebody who walks behind the rows, and they really won't shut up about him – going as far as making ten movies about him!

Gein, Edward - An American murderer also known as The Butcher of Plainfield. Despite his serial killer reputation, Gein only confessed to killing two women. His notoriety stems more from his rather unusual and macabre hobby of digging up dead people from the local cemetery and fashioning various household objects out of them, as well as items of clothing. He was the inspiration behind a number of seminal horror creations including Norman Bates in *Psycho*, Leatherface in *The Texas Chain Saw Massacre* and Buffalo Bill in *The Silence of the Lambs*. He died of cancer in 1984. And, as far as I know, nobody dug *him* up.

Gemini Killer (James Venamun) – A deceased serial killer who wound up possessing Father Damien Karras in The Exorcist III. He enjoys Shakespeare, lobbing people's index fingers off, and showmanship.

One time he cut off someone's head and held it up so they could see their decapitated body – a little extra he threw in for no added charge. What a nice man.

Gévaudan Beast - The Beast of Gévaudan was a very real and documented series of attacks in France between 1764 and 1767 by what is speculated by some to be a werewolf. In reality, it was probably just a very large wolf or a pack of wolves. The beast killed over 100 people before finally being slain by Jean Chastel with a silver bullet (so it probably was a werewolf, then) in 1767. The 2001 French horror movie, *Brotherhood of the Wolf*, is based on the attacks.

Ghost - The apparition of a dead person, either that someone actually sees or feels the presence of. The horror genre is riddled with ghosts owing to a collective interest in life after death shared by a large portion of the population. In horror films, ghosts are usually malevolent spirits who have experienced some kind of turmoil in life and have returned to spoil everything for the nice family who have just bought a new house at a very good price. They can often be awakened by a séance or a Ouija board and tend to reside in spooky old houses or in hotels. Notable movies include: *The Shining, The Amityville Horror, The Haunting, Poltergeist, The Conjuring, The Sixth Sense* and *The Changeling*.

Ghostbuster - The term for someone who exterminates or captures ghosts for containment - although those contained ghosts are likely to be let loose by pencil-pushing bureaucrats.

Ghostface (or Ghost Face; GhostFace) - The central killer in the *Scream* movies, though unlike most movie bogeymen, Ghostface is never the same person behind the mask. Ghostface always dresses in a black robe with an elongated white mask and utilizes a voice changer so that, no matter who is taking on his/her identity, they always sound the same – and indeed Ghostface was always voiced by the same voice actor, Roger L. Jackson. The now iconic ghostly white mask was inspired by Edvard Munch's 1893 *The Scream* painting.

Ghoulies - Small, monstrous, demonic creatures that feature in the film series of the same name. Often considered to be a *Gremlins* rip-off (though both films were in production at the same time) the Ghoulies were the stars of four feature films. They come in various shapes and sizes, but their most iconic image is immortalized on the film's theatrical poster with one of the creatures sitting in a toilet bowl, emblazoned with the tagline, "They'll get you in the end!" Classic.

Ghouls - Alternative name for zombies. Notably George Romero's zombies were referred to as ghouls in his seminal 1968 movie *Night of the Living Dead*. The word is derived from an 18th century Arabic word, "ghūl" – which is an evil spirit that robs graves and eats corpses.

Giallo - A horror movie sub-genre that hails from Italy and tends to feature a murder-mystery storyline, stylized violence, lots of color, a groovy music score, a killer wearing black gloves, and lots of bloody murders. Italian film director Dario Argento is perhaps the director most heavily associated with the subgenre, with films such as *The Bird with the Crystal Plumage*, *Deep Red* and *Tenebrae* being classic examples of the style. The word actually means "yellow" in Italian – the significance of the color being the yellow-covered *Il Giallo Mondadori* mystery paperback novels that inspired the genre.

Gill-man - The humanoid amphibian featured in *Creature from the Black Lagoon* and its two sequels, *Revenge of the Creature* and *The Creature Walks Among Us*. Gill-man (sometimes simply referred to as "The Creature") has webbed hands, with sharp claws on each finger, very tough skin, an ability to heal fast and can breathe both in and out of water. Gill-man doesn't like people hanging around his lagoon and so tends to kill them, rather than asking them to politely leave. And he's rather fond of the ladies. As well as appearing in the Universal Monster's trilogy of films, he also features in *The Monster Squad* (1987).

Gingerdead Man (Millard Findlemyer) – He sure ain't the Pillsbury f**king doughboy, he says. The Gingerdead Man is a bit like Chucky from the *Child's Play* films in that after he was killed his soul was transferred into another object. But instead of a creepy doll, it was a put into a gingerbread man. Sounds a bit far-fetched.

Gizmo - The central Mogwai creature featured in the two *Gremlins* movies. His owner is Billy Peltzer, a man who really should have never been allowed to look after such a volatile animal… twice!

Glen Echo - The fictional town featured in *Behind the Mask: The Rise of*

Goblin (band) - An Italian progressive rock band best known for providing the soundtracks to a number of classic Italian horror movies – most notably Dario Argento's movies *Deep Red* and *Suspiria.*

God - Another word for Freddy Krueger's glove. Well, according to him, at least.

Godzilla - A huge, monstrous, amphibious prehistoric reptile, also known as the King of the Monsters and created in Japan by Toho Co., Ltd. Godzilla was awakened by nuclear testing in the 1950s and in the many motion pictures he has appeared in he is always portrayed as a bipedal reptilian with rows of leaf-shaped dorsal plates down his back. Over the years he has had plenty of fights with other monsters (including King Kong) and generally likes to stomp over everything and cause a big mess.

Good Guys - A brand of doll produced by the Play Pals toy company. Good Guys were inspired by a fictional popular TV cartoon series and the original doll was advertised as being able to say three phrases, move its head and blink its eyes. Although it does a lot more than that in the *Child's Play* movies. A *hell* of a lot more.

Gore - A word used to describe the graphic special effects makeup featured in horror movies. Gore effects are usually achieved by using lots of fake blood and prosthetic makeup.

Gothic horror - A subgenre of horror film usually set in the past and often based upon a literary work of Gothic fiction. Gothic horror movies tend to focus upon themes of romanticism, the supernatural and the murderous set within areas of gothic architecture with period costume designs. Some notable examples of Gothic horror include *Bride of Frankenstein* (1935), *Bram Stoker's Dracula* (1992), *Interview with the Vampire* (1994), *The Others* (2001) and *Sleepy Hollow* (1999).

Graboid - A large worm-like subterranean creature featured in the *Tremors* movies and TV series. Graboids are attracted to sound and, should one of them hear you shuffling around on the surface above them, they are likely to burst through the ground and gobble you up.

Grady girls - They want to play with you, forever and ever and ever.

Grand Guignol - The name of a Parisian theatre that, between 1897 and 1962, was known for staging gory and violent horror shows. Its full title was Le Théâtre du Grand-Guignol, which translates to The Theatre of the Great Puppet. The term Grand Guignol has now become a phrase used to describe dramatic entertainment of a particularly graphic or horrific nature.

Gravers - Undead humans that are created and under the control of The Tall Man in the *Phantasm* film franchise; similar to Lurkers, but not squashed. Often Gravers wear gas masks and are tasked with digging up the recently deceased to aid The Tall Man in his rather strange endeavors.

Green Man Inn - A local tavern on Summerisle where the inhabitants are prone to bursting into song for no other reason than to creep out outsiders who drop in for a pint. *See The Wicker Man (1973), but don't see The Wicker Man (2006)…* ever!

Gremlin - The small, monstrous offspring of a Mogwai that spawn from a cocoon. Gremlins are a reptilian creature hellbent on causing chaos and destruction and having a really good time whilst doing so. Sunlight is their main nemesis. They feature in the films *Gremlins* and *Gremlins 2: The New Batch*. Generally, a gremlin is the name for any little monstrous creature that causes aircraft or other machines to malfunction.

Grindhouse - A term for a movie theater in America that screened lower budget exploitation films in continuous succession. The word has since gone on to be used to describe the type of films that were shown in the Grindhouse theaters. Typically, grindhouse films were low budget horror movies known to feature sex, gore, nudity and violence.

Grimm Brothers - The writers of all the stories that used to scare us as children.

Grim Reaper - The personification of death. The Grim Reaper is the rather miserable cloaked chap with the scythe that is coming for us all one day, regardless of whether or not we ate the salmon mousse.

Grizzly bear - A large type of omnivorous brown bear, also known as the North American Brown Bear. They do appear quite cuddly, but if you encounter one in a horror movie, it's likely to rip you to pieces. Notable examples: *Grizzly* (1976), Day of the Animals (1977), *Blackfoot Trail* (aka *Backcountry*) (2014) and *Into the Grizzly Maze* (2015).

Groovy - The iconic word Bruce Campbell's Ash Williams first utters in *Evil Dead II* (1987) after attaching a chainsaw to his severed hand. It is very groovy, to be fair.

Gunther - The name of the freakish funhouse monster featured in Tobe Hooper's 1981 film, *The Funhouse*. Gunther has sharp animal-like teeth, deformed facial features and spooky red eyes, making him perfect for a scary funhouse.

Gwoemul - The name of the large mutated amphibious creature in the Han River featured in the 2006 film *The Host*. Gwoemul was the result of formaldehyde pollution, turning the unknown host creature (possibly some kind of tadpole) into a ravenous, people-chopping monster. Gwoemul doesn't like fire, so they set it on fire and stabbed it with a metal pole. Problem solved.

H

Haddonfield - A fictional Illinois town featured in the majority of the *Halloween* movies. Aside from the murderous Michael Myers stalking and killing people on Halloween night, it's a pretty idyllic place. Perhaps book a vacation around that time if you plan to move there. The first movie, and some of the sequels were actually shot in South Pasadena, California.

Halloween - A celebration held on the 31st of October in which children (and adults, if you're like me) get dressed up in fancy-dress costumes to go trick-or-treating. Other activities include, having costume parties, carving pumpkins, lighting bonfires, apple bobbing, playing pranks, going to haunted attractions or places, watching horror movies and (if you're an escaped psychopath) killing people engaging in the above activities. Halloween features in countless horror films but is perhaps most well-known for being the central celebration in the *Halloween* film franchise.

Hammer Film Productions - A British film production company founded in 1934 that was famous for making (mostly) gothic horror feature films (and TV shows). *The Quatermass Xperiment* (1955) (known as *The Creeping Unknown* in the US) is regarded as the first of Hammer's horror movies, though it is arguably their foray into the world of classic movie monsters that was responsible for their reputation as a key horror filmmaking studio. Much like the Universal Classic Monsters, Hammer Film Productions churned out multiple movies featuring Dracula, Frankenstein and The Mummy, as well as a wealth of other popular horror movie villains. Production died-off in the late 70s but was revived in 2007, scoring a notable hit with the 2012 film, *The Woman in Black*.

Happy Toyz Truck - The main evil truck (also known as the Green Goblin Truck) featured in the 1986 Stephen King movie, *Maximum Overdrive*. The truck, along with a whole host of other machines, becomes possessed after the Earth passes through the tail of a comet. Lots of people get killed to the tunes of AC/DC before the Earth passes out of the comet's tail. The Happy Toyz Truck didn't make it to the end of the machine killing spree, though, having been destroyed by a rocket fired by Emilio Estevez.

Hårga – The name of a Swedish cult whose members are more than happy to leap of a cliff face to their gory demises when they reach the age of 72. They also enjoy ritualistic sacrifices. Not the best choice of location for a holiday.

Haunted - Any place that is frequented by a ghost or a group of ghosts.

Haunted house - Sometimes regarded as more of a subgenre of horror movie, haunted houses feature rather predominately in horror films and can quite often be based upon true stories. Some of the more notable haunted house movies include: *The Amityville Horror* (1979), *The*

Changeling (1980) and *The Innocents* (1961).

Head - The area of the human body that it is most effective to shoot a zombie in to "kill" it. Used in a sentence: "If you had a gun, shoot 'em in the head" (*Night of the Living Dead*). Of course, it doesn't always work, as was the case in *The Return of the Living Dead* in which the characters Frank and Freddy concluded that the movie (*Night of the Living Dead*) lied.

Head on a stick - The torture method used by Mick Taylor in *Wolf Creek*. Basically, take one large knife, add an unwilling victim, chop a couple of fingers off (optional), severe the victim's spine and… voila! You've got yourself a head on a stick!

Headstone - A chunk of stone that is used to mark the final resting place of a dead person, emblazoned with the name and a few titbits of info about the grave's deceased inhabitant. In *Halloween* (1978), Michael Myers thought it would be rather hilarious to take the headstone from his sister's grave and place it next to the body of one of his victims.

Hell – When there's no more room in it, the dead are scheduled to walk the Earth.

Helsing, Abraham Van - A fictional character originally featured in Bram Stoker's *Dracula* novel. Abraham Van Helsing is a vampire hunter whose main nemesis is Count Dracula. The character has appeared in countless adaptations of *Dracula* (and in other non-Dracula horror films too) but his most famous portrayal is arguably by Peter Cushing in the Hammer Horror movies.

Henrietta, Knowby - The name of a lady in *Evil Dead II* who is very protective of the fruit cellar she resides in, having been possessed by a Kandarian demon. Despite her malevolence, she has a very sweet swinging voice.

Henry - The name of the serial killer featured in the notorious 1986 movie *Henry: Portrait of a Serial Killer*. Henry, portrayed by Michael Rooker, was said to be based on the real life serial killer Henry Lee Lucas.

Hide and Clap - A game that it's not advisable to play in a haunted house.

Hill House - The titular building featured originally in Shirley Jackson's classic 1959 novel, *The Haunting of Hill House*. Its most famous appearance in the movies is in the 1963 horror flick *The Haunting*, though more recently the house opened its doors again in the Netflix TV series, *The Haunting of Hill House* (2018). There was also a 1999 film adaptation, but we'll brush over that. Needless to say, the large mansion house, in an undisclosed location, is riddled with ghosts who have the power to possess visitors and provoke them to kill themselves.

Hills - In Nevada, they are said to have eyes.

Hitchhiker - An entertaining, though kinda weird, young man picked up on a road in Texas by a group of friends. The hitchhiker (portrayed by Ed Neal) loves head cheese, photography, self-harm, cannibalism and murder. His real name is said to be Nubbins Sawyer.

Hitchhiking - The practice of flagging down cars for the purpose of being given a free ride. Hitchhiking is a rather dangerous thing to do in horror movies as it tends to be a serial killer at the wheel. Alternatively, the person hitchhiking is the psychotic one. Basically, just try to completely avoid hitchhiking.

Hobbling - The name of the procedure inflicted upon Paul Sheldon by Annie Wilkes in *Misery* (1990). According to Wilkes, hobbling was a method of stopping workers at the Kimberley Diamond Mines from running off with the goods. Annie's method of hobbling involves placing a large chunk of wood in between the patient's feet, swinging a large sledgehammer against both of them one at a time and topping it all off by announcing to the screaming recipient, "God, I love you." She has a funny way of showing it.

Hobb's End - The name of the town featured in John Carpenter's *In the Mouth of Madness* (1994). Within the film, Hobb's End features as the fictional location that is written about in the novels of horror writer Sutter Cane… who is also fictional.

Hobgoblins - A small, malevolent creature, rather like a gremlin. Well… in fact, exactly like a gremlin. Features in *Hobgoblins* (1988) and *Hobgoblins 2* (2009).

Hockey mask - The mask-of-choice for Jason Voorhees. Obtained by Jason in *Friday the 13th Part III* from the joker-in-the-pack character Shelly (played by Larry Zerner). Hockey masks have since become synonymous with murderous madmen… and Clark Griswold.

Holy Water - Water that has been blessed by a religious figure. Vampires tend not to like it. To really piss one off, try splashing some in their face.

Home invasion movie - A subgenre of horror film in which a person or family's home is intruded upon by either a single malevolent person or a group of them. Often the invasion can have a more innocent beginning with the invader or invaders being invited into the particular home and events slowly spiraling out of control, or it can be more sinister from the onset with the inhabitants being taunted by an unknown source that will eventually be revealed to them. Lots of violence tends to be involved. Some notable movies include *Funny Games* (1997/2008), *The Strangers* (2008), *You're Next* (2011), *Straw Dogs* (1971) and *Hush* (2016). A fun twist on the subgenre occurred with the 2016 movie *Don't Breathe*, in which the home-invaders realized that the house's inhabitant was far worse than they were.

Homicide - The American term for intentionally killing another person. Horror movies examples: A hell of a lot of horror movies.

Hook - A curved tool, usually made of metal that has multiple appearances in various styles in horror films. Most commonly hooks feature as either a substitute for a missing hand, or to hang people on.

Horror conventions - A gathering of horror fans, celebrities, merchandisers and cosplayers at a preselected venue and usually taking place over a weekend at a ticketed event. Members of the public are able to personally meet horror film and TV stars, get autographs and photographs and generally have a most excellent time in the surroundings of their peers. Often there will also be Q&A sessions with the special guests, as well as many other horror-related attractions.

Some of the biggest horror conventions include Monsterpalooza, Texas Frightmare Weekend, HorrorHound Weekend and HorrorConUK's Something Wicked.

Horror host - The name of a presenter who introduces horror films and cheesy B-movies in a humorous and often quite camp style on television or on the internet. Vampira is regarded as the first horror host and Elvira, Mistress of the Dark is considered the most well-known.

Hospital - A building in which sick or injured people are treated. In real-life they're always busy-as-hell and you have to wait hours to be seen. In horror movies they tend to be completely deserted. Scary things tend to happen in hospitals in horror movies. Notable examples: *Halloween II (1981)*, *Re-Animator (1985)*, *Visiting Hours* (1982) and *X-Ray* (aka *Hospital Massacre*) (1981).

Hostel - A cheap place for accommodation. Not advisable to stay in one in Slovakia.

House - A building used for the purposes of human habitation. "House" is a common word in horror film titles. Some horror movie examples include: *House* (1985), *House of the Dead* (2003), *House on Haunted Hill* (1959/1999), *House of Wax* (1953/2005), *House of 1000 Corpses* (2003) and *The House of the Devil* (2009). Houses in horror movies, more often than not, contain ghosts.

House Shark - A rather rare type of great white shark that seems to be able to survive on the land – specifically inside a house. Features in the 2017 movie, *House Shark*.

Howdy, Captain - Another name for the demon Pazuzu featured in *The Exorcist* movies and TV show. He sounds quite friendly though.

Human Centipede - The grotesque creation of a German surgeon who joins together, mouth-to-anus, three unwilling (obviously) tourists to create his very own living human centipede. Not content with just one vile movie about the subject, director Tom Six thought a sequel in which twelve people are joined together would be a fun idea too. And then, clearly now hooked on movies about human centipedes, he upped the ante even further and joined 500 people together. Let's hope this movie series doesn't go all *Friday the 13th* on us – although I could see a sequel set in space, joining together a thousand aliens, as quite an entertaining movie (title suggestion: *The Alien Centipede*).

Hybrid monster - A creature that has been created out of two separate animal breeds. Some of the more ludicrous monster hybrid movies include: *Piranhaconda* (2012), *Dinocroc* (2004), *SharkMan* (2005), *Mansquito* (2005), *Sharktopus* (2010), *Sharktopus vs. Pteracuda* (2014) and *Sharktopus vs. Whalewolf* (2015).

Hyde, Mr. - The name of the malevolent alter-ego of Dr. Henry Jekyll who becomes unleashed after drinking a potion of his own creation – primarily. As time goes on, Edward Hyde would also manifest whenever Jekyll was weak. *See also "Jekyll (Dr.)."*

Hypnosis - A method in which a person is put into an almost trance-like state in which they are able to recount experiences that may have been repressed. It's often used in horror films on characters who have experienced some type of trauma so that we, the viewer, can enjoy seeing their disturbing memories.

I

Igor - The name of the character who generically appears as a lab assistant in gothic horror movies. Despite Igor's association with the *Frankenstein* story, there is no lab assistant, or even a character named Igor in Mary Shelley's original novel. In the first Universal *Frankenstein* movie, the lab assistant was named Fritz, though in subsequent films in the series there was a character named Ygor, but he wasn't a lab assistant. Typically, Igor is portrayed as having a hunchback and is somewhat dimwitted. It is more likely that the stereotypical portrayal of Igor was in the 1974 Mel Brooks parody film, *Young Frankenstein*, played by Marty Feldman.

Imhotep - The name of an Egyptian High Priest who was mummified whilst still alive (*ouch!*) and resurrected after someone read aloud from the Scroll of Thoth in the classic 1932 Universal Horror movie *The Mummy*, portrayed by the iconic Boris Karloff. Whilst resurrected, Imhotep renamed himself Ardeth Bey and pretended to be an Egyptian archaeologist. When it transpired that Ardeth was intending to make a living mummy partner for himself, he was destroyed along with the magical scroll. Similar Imhotep hijinks featured in the 1999 remake of the same name, but it all got a bit Indiana Jonesy.

Indian burial ground - A Native American cemetery that is often associated with the horror genre. There appear to be some truths in how building over them can lead to supernatural events – Lake Shawnee Amusement Park in West Virginia, which opened in 1926, was built over an Indian burial ground and encountered six deaths before its closure in 1966. Notable Indian burial ground horror movies include: *The Amityville Horror* (1979), The Shining (1980), *Poltergeist II: The Other Side* (1986) and *Pet Sematary* (1989).

Invisible Man -

Invisibility - As the "Invisible Man" entry above was a very childish attempt at humor, I will address that particular horror movie monster here instead. The Invisible Man was the invention of H. G. Wells, in his 1897 novel of the same name, and concerns the story of Dr. Jack Griffin who goes a bit loopy after inventing a potion for making himself invisible and neglecting to make an antidote for it. Things get out of hand and he ends up killing various people before being killed himself. Perhaps the most famous adaptation remains James Whale's 1933 film starring Claude Rains as the Invisible Man. Aside from Universal's *The Invisible Man* and its sequels, invisibility hasn't played a large part in the horror genre, with perhaps *Hollow Man* (2000) being one of its most notable, erm… appearances.

It - Something that relentlessly follows you in various guises until you are dead.

J

Jack-o'-lantern - A hollowed-out pumpkin with a face carved into and a light put inside. The name is thought to have come from the legend of Stingy Jack, who was an Irish drunkard (obviously) who tricked the Devil and eventually was considered such a unsavory character that God wouldn't allow him into Heaven, and the Devil, upset at being repeatedly tricked by Jack, wouldn't let him into Hell either, but he gave him an ember from the fires of hell, which Jack put into a hollowed-out turnip to light his way. Stingy Jack is said to still roam the Earth to this day. It might be a bit difficult to find him on Halloween night, though.

Japanese horror (J-horror) - A horror movie produced in Japan that usually features ghosts, the supernatural, poltergeists and elements of Japanese folk religion. They can also feature rather brutal violence and heavy scenes of gore. Perhaps some of the most well-known J-horror movies are *Ring* aka *Ringu* (1998), *Ju-On: The Grudge* (2002), *Dark Water* (2002), *Audition* (1999) and *Battle Royale* (2000).

Jarvis, Tommy - The most reoccurring character from the *Friday the 13th* movies, aside from Jason (and his mom). Tommy is one of the rare examples of a Final Boy in slasher movies and has survived three encounters with Jason Voorhees (well, one of them was a copycat Jason). He also made a fourth appearance in the extended fan-made film, *Never Hike Alone* (2017), played again by Thom Mathews who portrayed the character in *Friday the 13th Part VI: Jason Lives*.

Jaws rip-offs – Something of a mini sub-genre, particularly popular in the wake of the 1975 hit, *Jaws*. Jaws rip-offs didn't necessarily have to be about sharks; keen to cash-in on Spielberg's success, filmmakers chose various other predators as the film's monstrous villains – Bears (*Grizzly*), Octopuses (Tentacles), Killer Whales (*Orca*), Alligators (*Alligator*) and Piranhas (*Piranha*). As you can tell, no one got particularly creative with the titles.

Jekyll, Dr. - The more sensible one in the Jekyll and Hyde partnership. Dr. Henry Jekyll is conflicted between good and evil and so invents a serum to repress his evil thoughts, unfortunately the potion brings out his evil side. So, basically, after drinking he becomes violent (you can tell this story was written by a Scotsman).

Jigsaw - A type of puzzle in which an image, printed onto wood or cardboard, is cut up into various shapes that have to be reassembled by somebody with too much spare time on their hands. In the 1982 film, *Pieces*, the killer chopped out jigsaw-shaped pieces from his victims and pieced them together to create an incredibly grisly jigsaw-corpse. Except, it isn't really a corpse, it's alive! And then it goes and castrates someone! *Huh?! What?!* Yeah, there were a lot of drugs going around in the eighties.

Joint - A rolled cannabis cigarette often smoked by characters known as "stoners" in horror movies. Joints are often passed around in horror movies and partaking in smoking one often leads to a very quick and brutal death.

Josef - The name of a serial killer, who's a bit of creep. Josef likes having people film his day-to-day activities whilst also trying to scare the bejesus out of them. Portrayed by Mark Duplass in the films *Creep* (2014) and *Creep 2* (2017).

Judas Breed – A hybrid bug created from termite and mantis DNA. They were designed with good intentions, but someone went and put them in a horror film, so, naturally bad stuff happened. Their hobbies include mimicking people and killing them.

Jump-scare - A technique used in horror films to make the audience leap out of their seats, or at least jump a bit. A jump-scare is usually orchestrated with a sudden on-screen movement or appearance of either a character or animal or object, accompanied by an abrupt sound or a shocking piece of music. They are often overused in modern horror movies to the point where viewers become rather desensitized to them, but, if edited together correctly and with an effective choice of sound or music, they can still be effective. The hand-from-the-grave at the end of *Carrie* (1976) is often considered one of the first (and best) jump-scares. Other notable jump-scares include Jason emerging from Crystal Lake in *Friday the 13ᵗʰ* (1980) and the jolting moment in *The Exorcist III* (1990) with the nurse in the corridor.

K

Kandarian Demon - An ancient demonic spirit featured in the *Evil Dead* movies and TV shows. Kandarian demons really love swooshing through the woods making a loud rumbling sound. And I think we all love that about them too.

Kane, Reverend Henry - The name of the human-form of The Beast in the *Poltergeist* movies. The jovial, but frankly weird, Reverend Kane first appears in *Poltergiest II: The Other Side* and was portrayed by the terminally ill 60-year-old actor Julian Beck, who died shortly after filming.

Kensington, Gore - The name given to the fake blood recipe created by pharmacist John Tynegate – named after an area in London. It traditionally consisted of Golden Syrup (light treacle), food colorants red, yellow and blue, water, corn flour (corn starch) and peppermint extract (so it had a nice minty taste for actors using it orally). It was predominately used in Hammer Horror movies. Despite most filmmakers not using this particular formula anymore, the term Kensington Gore is often used to describe any type of theatrical blood.

Kergozu - The name of the demon featured in the story (*The Demon of Heritage*) at the end of this book. Okay, so it's not a horror movie... yet. Maybe someday. Here's some trivia anyway – I used to work for a company that made hearing aids and one day I saw that a client's name was Kergozu, and I thought it sounded like a great name for a demon! My apologies to whoever that person was. I'm sure you're really very nice.

Killer Klowns - A group of freaky clowns from outer space who like to eat humans (most things from outer space seem to like human meat – have none of them tried chicken?).

Killer scarecrows - A subgenre of horror film featuring nasty scarecrows killing people – usually in direct-to-video titles such as *Scarecrow* (2002), *Scarecrow Slayer* (2003), *Scarecrow Gone Wild* (2004), *Dark Harvest* (2004), *Hallowed Ground* (2007), *Husk* (2011) and *Curse of the*

Scarecrow (2018). Superior to all of those movies is the 1981 TV movie, considered the first in the subgenre, *Dark Night of the Scarecrow*.

Knife - A sharp, metal object featured prominently throughout many horror movies, particularly slasher movies. Arguably, the horror movie icon most associated with knives is Michael Myers from the *Halloween* movies, who favors a really big, sharp kitchen knife.

Komodo Dragon - A huge and rather monstrous predatory lizard from the Indonesian islands Rinca, Flores, Gill Motang, Padar and, of course, Komodo. Human attacks are roughly about as rare as horror films featuring Komodo dragons. The most notably is probably the 1999 film *Komodo*, but they have also featured in a couple of direct-to-video titles, namely *The Curse of the Komodo* (2004) and *Komodo vs. Cobra* (2005).

Krampus - The antithesis of Santa Claus; Krampus punishes naughty children instead of rewarding good children. He's known to go a bit far with his punishments, for example: drowning, eating or taking them to hell, but most of the time he just hits them with sticks. His usual appearance is that of a horned, hairy beast with cloven hooves. Notable movies: *Krampus* (2015) and *A Christmas Horror Story* (2015).

Krueger, Freddy (Frederick Charles Krueger) - The main antagonist in the *A Nightmare on Elm Street* film franchise. Freddy was a child murderer before being burned to death by the angry parents of his victims. But not one to let a little touch of death bother him, he continued to kill the youngsters of Springwood by invading their dreams and killing them in a variety of horrific, but imaginative, ways. Freddy Krueger was portrayed by Robert Englund in the first seven movies (and TV spin-off) and by Jackie Earle Haley in the 2010 remake. Freddy Krueger's hobbies include making razor-blade gloves, self-harm, quipping, consuming souls, murder and starring in sequels.

L

Lake Placid - A rather calm, picturesque lake in Maine that is home to a giant man-eating crocodile. Its size and appetite are the result of one of *The Golden Girls* overfeeding it.

La Llorona - A ghost in Latin American folklore, also known as The Weeping Woman. La Llorona is the tale of a lady who drowned her two children in a blind rage after being spurned by her husband. When she came to her senses, she vainly searched the river for days before being found dead herself on the riverbank. Her spirit kidnaps and drowns children wandering around at night and hearing her cries can bring both misfortune and death. The 2006 Mexican horror film, *Kilometer 31*, is inspired by the tale as well as the 2019 film *The Curse of La Llorona* from *The Conjuring* Universe.

Lambton Worm - A British legend concerning a giant dragon-like worm that terrorized villages around the River Wear in North East England. The name derives from John Lambton who caught the creature whilst fishing. It was only a small eel-like creature primarily, which Lambton ditched in a well. Many years later the worm returned and after causing much trouble was captured by Lambton who initially kept it as a pet, feeding it large quantities of milk every day. When supplies were becoming rather depleted, he killed the worm, after a lengthy fight. Bram Stoker's 1911 novel, *The Lair of the White Worm* and its 1988 film adaptation are based upon the legend.

Lament Configuration - The name of the puzzle box featured in the *Hellraiser* films. Within the *Hellraiser* movie universe, the box was created by a young French toymaker named Philip Lemarchand for his wealthy client, Duc de L'Isle. In the first film it is successfully opened by Frank Cotton, who didn't really mind if it opened the door to heaven or hell. Being a horror movie, obviously it took him to hell where he met a bunch of questionably dressed cenobites who ripped him to pieces. In retrospect, he'd have preferred the heaven option.

Lamia - The name of the demon featured in Sam Raimi's *Drag Me to Hell* (2009). The Lamia does various annoying things to its chosen victim for three days before finally dragging them down to hell. It's known as the most feared of all demons, which probably has a lot to do with the fact that there seems to be no way out of its goal of taking you to hell for all eternity. If you work in a bank, perhaps reconsider extending loan repayments to creepy-looking elderly women.

Lane, **Mandy** - A girl all the boys love. She's a killer, though, so maybe find someone else to swoon over.

Lavalantula – A swarm of lava-breathing tarantulas that like to fight against actors from the *Police Academy* movies.

Lawnmower - A mechanical device for trimming grass that is also rather effective at slaying large quantities of the undead. Lawnmowers occasionally also feature in slasher movies as a particularly nasty device for slaying victims. Weirdly, the 1992 horror film *The Lawnmower Man* completely missed a trick and chose to focus on virtual reality instead of having a demented killer slaughtering everybody with a lawnmower – you'll have to watch the 1982 horror comedy *Wacko* for that.

Leatherface - The central killer in *The Texas Chain Saw Massacre* (and sequels, prequels and remake). His nickname refers to the masks he wears, made out of human skin. Depending on which movie in the canon you're viewing, his real name is either Jedidiah Sawyer, Thomas "Bubba" Sawyer, "Junior" Sawyer, "Leather" Slaughter or Thomas Brown Hewitt – maybe for somebody who wears such a wide variety of faces, it's only apt that he should have so many names. He doesn't say an awful lot, comes across as a bit simple, and despite the title of the franchise, doesn't always use a chainsaw to kill people (in *Texas Chainsaw Massacre: The Next Generation*, he doesn't kill *anyone* with a chainsaw). His most iconic portrayal is by Gunnar Hansen in the first movie. Leatherface's hobbies include cannibalism, embroidery, and dancing with chainsaws.

Lecter, Hannibal - Also known as the Chesapeake Ripper or Hannibal the Cannibal, Lecter originally appeared in Thomas Harris' 1981 novel *Red Dragon* and was first portrayed on film in the 1986 adaptation, *Manhunter*, by actor Brian Cox. However, it wasn't until Anthony Hopkins' Academy Award winning portrayal of Lecter in *The Silence of the Lambs* (1991) that he was fully embraced as an icon of horror. Dr. Hannibal Lecter's hobbies include psychiatry, cookery, hosting dinner parties, music, art, cannibalism and playful mind games (with a sinister undercurrent).

Leprechaun - A usually benign, gold-obsessed, little bearded man, dressed in green from Irish folklore. The *Leprechaun* film series feature a leprechaun who took his love of gold a bit too far, killing anyone who steals it.

Lestat - The name of the vampire in *Interview with the Vampire* (1994) portrayed by Tom Cruise (and also Stuart Townsend in *Queen of the Damned*). Lestat de Lioncourt was the creation of writer Anne Rice in her series of *The Vampire Chronicles* novels. He doesn't have much of a conscious when it comes to killing mortals for their blood. As he puts it himself, "God kills indiscriminately, and so shall we," which I suppose is a pretty good point really.

Leviathan - The lord of The Labyrinth in *Hellbound: Hellraiser II*, also known as the God of Flesh, Hunger and Desire. It's a big diamond-shaped object that hovers over The Labyrinth in the Cenobite's domain, making an annoying foghorn-like sound and shooting out beams of ominous black light. Fiddling around with a little puzzle box can easily thwart it, though.

Leviathan (shipwreck) – The name of deliberately shrunken soviet ship that RoboCop, one of the Sticky Bandits and a Ghostbuster salvaged back in the 80s (when there were a lot of sea monsters about). They drank some mutagen-spiked vodka (never a good idea) and Stan Winston showed up to build another one of his monsters.

Lipstick-Face Demon - An insidious demon (and Darth Maul lookalike) who likes to play with puppets, sharpen its nails and abduct children. The Lipstick-Face Demon, also known as the Red-Faced Demon, was portrayed in the *Insidious* film series by Joseph Bishara (who also composed the music for the films).

Loomis, Dr. Samuel - The name of Michael Myers' psychiatrist from the *Halloween* movies, portrayed by Donald Pleasence from 1978-1995 and Malcolm McDowell from 2007-2009. Loomis got fed up trying to make small-talk with Myers in the Smith's Grove Sanitarium and was probably the one who left the front gate open in the hope that the inevitable killing-spree would give them something to talk about.

Lotion - It rubs it on its skin. Then places it in the basket.

Lovecraftian - A subgenre of horror film, named after the American writer H. P. Lovecraft, and sometimes referred to as Cosmic Horror. It is typified by a merging of both horror with science fiction that questions the normal bounds of reality. Lovecraftian can also be a word used to describe other-worldly monstrous creatures.

Lubdan - The name of the evil, murderous, gold-obsessed leprechaun featured in the *Leprechaun* movies. Portrayed by Warwick Davis in the first six movies (1993-2003); Dylan 'Hornswoggle' Postl in *Leprechaun: Origins* (2014) and Linden Porco in *Leprechaun Returns* (2018). One of Lubdan's most endearing traits is his knack for speaking in rhymes, for example, "For pulling this trick, I'll chop off your dick!"

Lurkers - The shrunken corpses featured in the *Phantasm* movies, created and ruled by The Tall Man. Lurkers appear rather demonic and are always seen wearing cloaks, just like the Jawas in *Star Wars* (perhaps they're related?). They are usually sent to work as slaves on the red planet or are dispatched to attack anyone trying to thwart The Tall Man and his bizarre, grisly plans.

Lycanthrope - Another word for "werewolf," or a person who thinks they are a wolf. The word is derivative of the Greek words for wolf, "lykos," and human, "anthropos."

M

Macabre Mobile - A customized convertible Ford Thunderbird driven by Elvira (Cassandra Peterson) in *Elvira: Mistress of the Dark* (1988). It features a bat hood ornament, a spider-web grill, leopard skin upholstery and skull-and-crossbones hubcaps.

Machete - A very large knife that's supposed to be used for cutting trees or plants, but mostly gets used as a weapon in horror films — there's not really much of an audience for lengthy scenes of garden cultivation. The machetes' most famous horror movie owner is probably Jason Voorhees from the *Friday the 13th* movies.

Macneil, Regan - The name of the young girl who became possessed by a malevolent demon in Georgetown in the seventies. Her mother first thought things were a little off with her when she peed all over the floor during a party and told her astronaut friend that he was going to die in space. Thankfully things soon got sorted out and Regan's mom is really very sorry about the two exorcists that ended up dying during the whole kerfuffle.

Mad - Something we all go a little, sometimes.

Madhouse - An alternative name for a psychiatric hospital, lunatic asylum or mental institution. Also, the name of a 1981 Italian horror movie.

Mall - A large building filled with a lot of clothes to buy, a smattering of other types of stores and a whole bunch of eateries – and sometimes, zombies. Notable horror movies: *Dawn of the Dead* (1978/2004), *Chopping Mall* (1986), *The Initiation* (1984), *Sorority Babes in the Slimeball Bowl-O-Rama* (1988), and *Phantom of the Mall: Eric's Revenge* (1989).

Man - The warmest place to hide.

Mangler, The - A demonically possessed laundry folding machine at the Blue Ribbon Laundry in Riker's Valley. Aside from its normal launderette function, The Mangler is known to devour anybody who gets too close to it. Stephen King thought it up. Features in the films *The Mangler* (1995) and *The Mangler Reborn*, but not *The Mangler 2* (2002) – it went back to folding clothes for that one.

Maniac Cop - A psychotic killer who dresses in a police uniform and ensures that you have the right to remain silent... forever. Appears in the three movies, *Maniac Cop* (1988), *Maniac Cop 2* (1990) and *Maniac Cop III: Badge of Silence* (1993).

Mannequin - A life-sized human doll most often used to display clothing in department stores. Mannequins can quite often be found in horror movies on account of their resemblance to a living person. They're frequently used in scenes where a living person is hiding amongst them, or in a more supernatural way by moving around by themselves. Frank Zito (played by Joe Spinell in *Maniac*) nailed his victims' scalps onto them. Which was a bit weird. Notable appearances: *Tourist Trap* (1979), *Maniac* (1980 and 2012), *Pin* (1988), *Lights Out* (2016) and *Halloween* (2018).

Mariticide - The act of someone killing their husband. Notable horror movie example: *Dead Alive* aka *Braindead* (1992).

Mars - A planet where aliens come from.

Martian - The name given to any fictional alien being from the planet Mars. The aliens in *The War of the Worlds* came from Mars and, obviously, so did the ones in *Invaders from Mars*.

Mary, Bloody - An urban legend involving the saying of "Bloody Mary" into a mirror in the hope that she will appear and kill you. Historically, the saying of Bloody Mary's name (in varying repetitive amounts) will conjure either a friendly or evil apparition. Horror movies obviously tend to focus upon the nasty version. Notable film appearances: *Urban Legends: Bloody Mary* (2005), *Bloody Mary* (2006), *Dead Mary* (2007) and *The Legend of Bloody Mary* (2008). Clive Barker's *Candyman* also has some elements of the Bloody Mary legend.

Marz, Madman - Based on the urban legend of Cropsey, this axe-wielding maniac supposedly appears when his name is spoken above a whisper… and so some douchebag just *had* to shout it out, didn't he? Initially, Madman Marz killed his entire family with an axe, before being struck in the face with an axe himself and hung – although he escaped and ran off into the woods. In the 1981 slasher movie, *Madman,* he returns to kill a group of people at a summer camp.

Mask - A covering for the face, most commonly worn by psychopaths. Arguably one of the most iconic horror film masks is Michael Myers' expressionless white mask worn in the *Halloween* film series. For John Carpenter's original 1978 movie, the filmmakers simply turned a Captain Kirk *Star Trek* mask inside out, sprayed it white and widened the eyes. These days they have an army of people working on the masks and spend a small fortune designing and creating it – The best illustration of this getting totally out of hand was on *Halloween H20: 20 Years Later* (1998), which had multiple mask designs throughout the production, ultimately leading to expensive reshoots and even the inclusion of a CGI mask in some scenes where nobody could agree on which mask they liked best. Other notable masks: Jason Voorhees' Hockey mask in the *Friday the 13th* movies, Ghostface's mask in the *Scream* movies and Leatherface's mask(s) in *The Texas Chainsaw Massacre* movies.

Masonry Trowel - Makes a good stabbing device – especially if you're a young zombie girl who doesn't get along very well with your mother. Features in *Night of the Living Dead* (1968).

Massacre - The act of killing a whole bunch of people. The word is quite the frequent-flyer in horror movie titles. Some examples include: *The Texas Chain Saw Massacre* (1974), *The Slumber Party Massacre* (1982), *Mountaintop Motel Massacre* (1983) and *Drive In Massacre* (1976).

Matricide - The act of someone killing their own mother. Notable horror movie example: *Psycho* (1960).

Meat hook - A hook typically used by butchers to hang meat on. Technically, Leatherface in *The Texas Chain Saw Massacre* was just using it for its designated purpose… although the meat was still alive. And human.

Megalodon - A massive great white shark that lived millions of years ago and might still be alive today, hiding in the depths of the Mariana Trench.

Melt movies - A sub-genre of horror film in which (usually) practical special effects are utilized to show characters melting in lots of gooey, gory detail. Notable examples include: *The Incredible Melting Man* (1977), *Body Melt* (1993), *Street Trash* (1987) and *The Blob* (1988).

Merman - Though only briefly appearing in the 2012 film *The Cabin in the Woods*, the Merman was a terrifying half-human, half-fish creature who eats people before shooting their blood up out of its blowhole. Apparently, the cleanup on them is a nightmare.

Merrin, Father Lankester - A notable exorcist whose main nemesis was a demon named Pazuzu, who loved screaming out Merrin's name just to freak him out. Merrin would shout back, "The power of Christ compels you!" over and over until Pazuzu had enough and killed him. He was most famously portrayed by Max von Sydow in *The Exorcist* (1973).

Micmac Indians - The tribe of American Indians mentioned in *Pet Sematary* (1989) who were responsible for the creation and original usage of the burial ground that has the power to bring the dead back to life. Presumably, back when they were using it, it worked properly.

Microwave - A type of oven that cooks or heats up food quickly. Very effective for cooking and killing gremlins too. In horror film history, microwaves have been the titular star of the show just one time, in the 1983 movie *Microwave Massacre*.

Midian - A fictional subterranean city where the monsters live. Midian seems to get bigger and bigger and more monstrous with every new cut of the movie. Features in Clive Barker's *Nightbreed* (1990).

Mike, Stuntman - The name of a death-proof-car-driving killer who likes to pick up pretty ladies in his spooky black vehicle (a Chevy Nova) to illustrate the fact that he's safely strapped in during a car crash, and they're not. Played by Kurt Russell in Quentin Tarantino's 2007 film *Death Proof*.

Miner, The – Also known as Harry Warden. Do NOT accept a box of chocolates from this man.

Mirror - A reflective surface that humans use to check their hair in, or shave, or apply make-up or to just admire themselves. They can also provide some amusement for animals. They can often be used in horror films to reveal that the killer or monster is behind one of the characters (shutting a bathroom cabinet door is used quite frequently for this effect). Mirrors can also play a more supernatural role, or act as a gateway to another dimension. In vampire movies they can be used to reveal if a character is a vampire or not. Notable horror movies: *Candyman* (1992), *Mirrors* (2008), *Oculus* (2013) and *The Mirror* (2014).

Mist - An atmospheric surface-based cloud, rather like fog – except it tends to be riddled with enormous freaky monsters.

Mockbuster - In an attempt to cash-in on more popular and (usually) bigger budget horror films, some independent studios release films with very similar-sounding names and promotional artwork. This is in the hope that lesser-informed members of the public will mistake the new DVD release they've just picked up at their local store (for a suspiciously low price) for the big budget studio film they saw advertised on TV the other night. Notable examples include *I Am Omega* (2007), *Snakes on a Train* (2006), *AVH: Alien vs. Hunter* (2007), *Paranormal Entity* (2009) and *When a Killer Calls* (2006).

Mogwai - A diminutive, cute and cuddly little creature hailing from the Orient (although the *Gremlins* novelization establishes that they are extraterrestrial in origin), which shouldn't really be sold to people at Christmastime. There are three main rules for looking after a Mogwai, all of which should be ignored if you wish to make a successful horror movie. Summarizing the three rules: 1) They don't like bright lights - sunlight will kill them, 2) Don't get them wet – this will cause them to multiple and produce weird or malevolent offspring and 3) Don't feed them after midnight – this will turn them into a really nasty, mean-spirited creature called a gremlin. Features in the films *Gremlins* and *Gremlins 2: The New Batch*. The word "mogwai" comes from a Cantonese word that means evil spirit, demon or monster.

Mohawk - The name of one of the main Gremlin creatures featured in *Gremlins 2: The New Batch*, supposedly the reincarnation of Stripe from the first movie.

Mokele-mbembe - The name of a dinosaur that still lives today in the Congo in Africa. The words roughly translate to "one who stops the flow of rivers." Appears in the 2012 movie *The Dinosaur Project*. I saw it once. *The Dinosaur Project* I mean, not Mokele-mbembe.

Mondo films - A type of exploitation documentary film that features a mix of genuine and staged footage, typically of a shocking nature. Arguably one of the most famous Mondo films is *Faces of Death* (1978) and its many sequels.

Monkeys Paw - A 1902 short story by W. W. Jacobs in which a severed monkey's paw has the power to give the owner three wishes. Being a horror tale, there's always ghastly consequences. For example, in the original story the paw's owner, Mr. White, wishes for £200 and the next day his son is killed in a factory accident, which profits him £200 in a goodwill payment from the employer. *Oops!* Clearly not learning from his mistake, he wishes he son back from the dead, and that pesky paw goes and brings him back all mutilated and decomposing. In summary… careful what you wish for. Notable horror film adaptations: *Tales from the Crypt* (1972), *Deathdream* (1974) and *The Monkey's Paw* (2013).

Monroeville Mall - The name of the real-life mall in Pennsylvania in which *Dawn of the Dead* (1978) was mostly filmed in.

Monster - An umbrella term for all types of creatures featured in horror films. Monsters can simply be human beings or various animals, alien beings, genetic mutations or hybrids or completely fictional creations.

Moon - The big round thing in the sky that can induce craziness in people when it's fully exposed. In most werewolf movies it also heralds the transformation from human into werewolf/wolfman.

Moonlight Man - The nickname given to a man named Raymond Andrew Joubert (sometimes also called the Space Cowboy). After a sex game goes terribly, terribly wrong, Gerald's wife, Jessie, who is handcuffed to the bed with her dead husband on the floor, thinks the Moonlight Man is a figment of her fevered imagination. It transpires he is very much a real person, and a pretty weird one at that. Features in the 2017 Stephen King adaptation, *Gerald's Game*.

Moors - Keep off them. Probably best to stick to the roads if you're backpacking in Yorkshire.

Morgan, Samara - *See "Sadako Yamamura."*

Morningside, Jebediah - The real name of The Tall Man featured in the *Phantasm* film franchise.

Morningside Mortuary - The name of the establishment in *Phantasm* where a man, known as The Tall Man (because he's rather tall, and a man) squashes the recently deceased and sticks them into barrels before sending them off to a red planet to become slaves. And we all were led to believe we were going to heaven when we died. No, apparently, as The Tall Man himself says, "You come to us!" Rotter.

Mosquito - An annoying insect that drinks blood and ends up killing over 750,000 people every year. Considering its prosperity as a human killer, you'd expect they would be more of a presence in horror movies, however, their most notable appearance is perhaps in the 1994 horror film starring Gunnar (Leatherface) Hansen aptly named *Mosquito*. Mosquitoes also have the ability to bring the dinosaurs back to life.

Motel - A roadside establishment where rooms can be rented for a short (yes, always short) length of time.

Mummy - A human (or animal) dead body that has been preserved after removing its internal organs and treated with various chemicals before being wrapped in bandages to await its return to life hundreds or thousands of years later. Mummies may not be the most ubiquitous horror movie monsters, but they are amongst the most iconic. The most well-known Mummy movies are arguably the Universal Monsters films (and also Hammer Films), though they have also featured in the movies *The Monster Squad* (1987), *Waxwork* (1988), *Tales from the Darkside: The Movie* (1990), *Bubba Ho-Tep* and, of course, the 2005 *Scooby-Doo* film, *Where's My Mummy*?

Murder - The act of intentionally killing another person. Murder features very heavily in horror movies, particularly in the slasher movie subgenre.

Musical adaptations - Though not particularly rampant, some popular horror films have been turned into stage musicals over the years, one of the earliest examples being the notorious Broadway flop, *Carrie* and one of the most successful being the adaptation of Roger Corman's 1960 film *The Little Shop of Horrors*, which was, of course, turned back into a film in 1986. They have proved more popular lately off-Broadway with such titles as *Evil Dead: The Musical, Re-Animator: The Musical, Silence! The Musical* and *The Toxic Avenger* all receiving acclaim from critics and audiences. Some rather amusing song titles include: Blew That Bitch Away (*Evil Dead: The Musical*), Thank God She's Blind (*The Toxic Avenger*) and If I Could Smell Her Cunt (*Silence! The Musical*).

Mutant - Something that has mutated from its natural form, usually caused by some type of human tinkering. Mutants in horror films tend to be deformed humans, like in *The Hills Have Eyes*, for example, or they can be mutated animals too, like the rabbits in *Night of the Lepus*.

Myers, Michael - The central killer in the *Halloween* film franchise. Named after Michael Myers from the British film distribution company Miracle Films. *Halloween* executive producer, (and the man who conceived of *The Babysitter Murders* concept that would later become *Halloween*) Irwin Yablans, named the bogeyman after Myers out of gratitude for him suggesting he enter *Assault on Precinct 13* into the London Film Festival, which in turn led to the successful UK distribution of the movie. In the *Halloween* movies, Michael Myers (or The Shape) began killing folk at the tender age of six, probably because he's just purely and simply evil. Michael enjoys meeting new people (to kill them), trick or treating, giving people the silent treatment, appearing in movies with a confused timeline and spending time with his family (to kill them). His favorite food is dog.

N

Nail gun - Cheaper than a chainsaw.

Nail, Rusty - The name of a trucker who can't really take a joke. Rusty Nail taunts his potential victims over a CB radio in the three *Joy Ride* movies: *Joy Ride* (2001), *Joy Ride 2: Dead Ahead* and *Joy Ride 3: Roadkill*. The movies are known as *Roadkill* in the UK, which technically should mean part three is called *Roadkill 3: Roadkill*.

Nards - A slang term for testicles. As concluded by Horace in *The Monster Squad* (1987), The Wolfman definitely *does* have them.

Necronomicon ex-mortis - Also known as the *Book of the Dead*. Written by the dark ones when the seas ran red with blood. The dark ones clearly took advantage of this abundance of blood and used it to ink the book. Reading passages from it tends to invoke a running-through-the-woods POV shot. Features predominately in the *Evil Dead* films as well as the *Ash vs Evil Dead* television series – it also makes an appearance in *Jason Goes to Hell: The Final Friday* (1993).

Necrophilia - A profound interest or sexual attraction to dead bodies. The word is derived from the Greek words for corpse (necro) and love (philia). The practice of necrophilia occasionally pops up as the main subject in horror movies, most notably in *Nekromantik* (1987) and *Nekromantik 2* (1991), but more usually it is featured in scenes for the shock-value, or even as a darkly comical sight-gag.

Night - The dark period of time that begins when the sun sets and ends when it rises. Plenty of terrible things occur during that period. It is also quite a common word used in horror movie titles – for example: *Night of the Living Dead* (1968), *Fright Night* (1985), *It Comes at Night* (2017), *Prom Night* (1980) and *Night of the Comet* (1984).

Nightmare - Another word for a scary dream. The word is derivative of the Old English word "Mare," which in Germanic and Slavic folklore is the name of a demon who sits on people's chests as they sleep, giving them frightening dreams. Arguably the most well-known usage of nightmares in horror films is in the *A Nightmare on Elm Street* film series, although they tend to crop up in a number of other horror films too, often tricking the viewer into believing they are merely watching a part of the film's narrative reality, when in fact it turns out to be a nightmare. And sometimes a nightmare, within a nightmare… within a movie, which we have nightmares about.

Nilbog - It's goblin spelled backwards! Features in *Troll 2* (1991).

Noodles - The vampire David from *The Lost Boys* can make you think they're worms. Party trick #1.

Nosferatu - Another word for "vampire" popularized by Bram Stoker's 1897 novel, *Dracula*, and the unauthorized film adaptation *Nosferatu* (1922). It is most commonly thought that the word is of Romanian origin, likely derivative of the Romanian words "nesuferit" (insufferable) and "necurat" (unclean spirit). However, it is also argued by some etymologists that the word came from the Greek "nosophoros," which means disease-bearing.

Nostromo (USCSS Nostromo) - A $42 million dollar spacecraft that was set to self-destruct by a particularly feisty female crew member after a malevolent alien creature boarded it. However, she did apologize… fifty-seven years later.

O

Oakley Court - A Victorian Gothic house in Bray, UK, where a number of horror films were shot, most notably by Hammer Film Productions. It is also famous for being The Frankenstein Place in *The Rocky Horror Picture Show* (1975). Oakley Court is currently a luxury hotel.

Occult - Knowledge and study of mysterious, magical, supernatural powers. The word derives from the Latin meanings for "Hidden" and "Secret." People who study the occult in horror movies tend to be a bit "spooky."

Oldsmobile (Delta 88) - A car (nicknamed "The Classic") featured, most prominently, in the *Evil Dead* movies and *Ash vs Evil Dead* TV series. The car, belonging to director Sam Raimi, has appeared in pretty much every one of his movies in some capacity.

Orca - The name of the fishing boat featured in *Jaws* (and as a sunken wreck in *Jaws 2*… and in some silly flashback scenes in *Jaws: The Revenge*). The Orca was owned by the rather unhinged local fisherman, Quint. Despite being a pretty good-sized boat, one of his passengers was quite vocal in complaining that it was too small.

Orlok, Count - The name of the fictional vampire based on Count Dracula, portrayed on film by German actor Max Schreck in the 1922 film *Nosferatu*, directed by F. W. Murnau. When the film was remade by Werner Herzog in 1979, as *Nosferatu the Vampyre*, the character was renamed Count Dracula and was portrayed by Klaus Kinski. In the 1988 sequel-of-sorts, *Vampire in Venice* (originally titled *Nosferatu a Venezia*), the character (again played by Kinski) was named Nosferatu.

Ouija Board - A flat board featuring letters of the alphabet, the numbers 0-9 and the words "yes," "no" and "goodbye." It's used for communicating with the dead or for just goofing around with after a few beers. Ouija boards, being a conduit for contacting dead folk, often find themselves in horror movies, sometimes central to the plot or often as either a catalyst for supernatural and horrific events that follow its use, or in an attempt to dispel a bothersome paranormal entity. Notable appearances: *The Exorcist* (1973), *Ouija* (2014), *Paranormal Activity* (2009), *Witchboard* (1986) and *The Conjuring 2* (2016).

Outpost 31 - The Antarctic research center featured in John Carpenter's *The Thing* (1982). Despite the characters referring to it as U.S. Outpost #31, the sign outside says, "United States National Science Institution Station 4." Perhaps all the mayhem caused by the shapeshifting lethal alien sneaking around in various guises led everyone to get a bit confused as to where they actually were.

Overlook Hotel - A secluded hotel in the Rocky Mountains. Avoid room 237. Or, if you're more of a bookworm, room 217.

Ozploitation - The name given to the spate of Australian low budget horror (and other genre) films that was birthed after the introduction of the R rating in 1971.

P

Paimon - The name of the demon featured in *Hereditary* (2018). Paimon, or King Paimon, is one of the kings of hell. The demon craves a male host, and after much harrowing shenanigans is finally granted one at the end of the film. My apologies if you haven't seen it already.

Paranormal - Something that is unexplainable by known science or nature. The paranormal is rampant in the horror genre and some film scholars would go so far as saying that true horror movies must always feature some element of the paranormal.

Paranormal Investigator - The name given to anyone who either professionally or on an amateur level looks into supposed cases of supernatural occurrences or activities.

Pazuzu - The name of the demon featured in *The Exorcist* movies and TV show. In ancient Mesopotamian religion, Pazuzu is seen as the king of the demons of the wind (but not farting). His statue looks friendly enough, though, with Pazuzu waving a friendly "hello," – although he does have a raging erection.

Pea soup - A substance that young girls are most likely to vomit if possessed by a demon.

Pennywise the Dancing Clown - The name of the rather creepy clown featured in Stephen King's *It*. Pennywise is only a manifestation of an ancient and malevolent being, often simply referred to as "IT." The clown guise *It* adopts is targeted to both lure, frighten and kill children – another name for *It* is "The Eater of Worlds." Pennywise the Dancing Clown doesn't tend to do an awful lot of dancing, although his usually jovial demeanor makes up for it. He was played by Tim Curry in the 1990 miniseries and by Bill Skarsgård in the *It: Chapter One* and *Two* (2017/2019) feature films.

Pentagram - A five-pointed star that can be found etched onto the wall in a Yorkshire pub, playfully named The Slaughtered Lamb. Don't make the mistake of asking the locals why it's there.

Perfection - A fictional small desert town first featured in the 1990 monster movie *Tremors*. According to the 2004 prequel *Tremors 4: The Legend Begins*, the town was originally named Rejection.

Phantasm - The illusion of a ghostly person or object – a figment of the mind, or apparition. The word is most popularly known in the horror genre as the title of a series of five films that don't really have much to do with the true definition of the word at all. It sounds cool though.

Phantom Killer - The name given to the unidentified serial killer whose crimes became known as the Texarkana Moonlight Murders. Eight people were attacked (five of whom were killed) in a ten-week period in Texarkana, Texas, in the spring of 1946. Nobody was ever caught. The 1976 horror movie, *The Town That Dreaded Sundown* (and the 2014 film of the same name) are based on the crimes.

Phantom of the Opera - The name given to the masked musical madman from the various versions of *The Phantom of the Opera*, whose real name is Erik Destler (which isn't quite as scary-sounding). Before Erik went off to become a Broadway star, he was more well-known as a horror movie character and appeared in two Universal Studios adaptations of the story, one with Lon Chaney as the titular star and the other with Claude Rains. The Phantom usually wears a white, half-face mask to hide his deformities and is besotted by the young opera singer Christine Daaé, often going as far as killing for her. Freddy Krueger once played the character in the 1989 horror film, *The Phantom of the Opera*.

Phibes, Anton - A rather abominable music and theology doctor, also known as Dr. Phibes, who was disfigured in a car crash that also damaged his voice. His new mission in life is to kill the doctors who he believed were responsible for the death of his sick wife. Just for an extra bit of fun, he utilizes the ten plagues of Egypt to orchestrate the deaths of the doctors. He is portrayed in the 1971 film by horror legend Vincent Price, who reprised the role in the 1972 sequel *Dr. Phibes Rises Again*.

Phillip, Black - A really nasty billy goat. Well, he is Satan in disguise, so I guess that's where the nastiness comes from. Features in *The VVitch* (2015).

Pieces – It's exactly what you think it is.

Pig blood - Ideal for plunging over the freaky girl in class at school proms. Check that she doesn't possess telekinetic powers first, though.

Pinhead - The lead cenobite (as he was first known) in the *Hellraiser* movies. Pinhead will tear your soul apart... as well as literally tearing you apart with all of his hooked chains he has dangling around the place. In life, Pinhead was a solider named Captain Elliot Spencer before messing with a puzzle box and having loads of pins shoved into his head (that almost never seems to happen with a Rubik's Cube). He is a cold, ruthless and sadistic demon and was chillingly portrayed by

Doug Bradley in the first eight *Hellraiser* movies.

Piranha - A type of South American fish with lots and lots of little sharp teeth to eat people with.

Pitchfork - An agricultural tool with a long handle and two or three curved metal prongs at the end. Sometimes used as a weapon in horror films (*The Prowler, Friday the 13th Part 2*) or by a group of angry villages who have ganged up to intimidate (or kill) someone monstrous they collectively don't get along with.

Plan - A group of aliens from outer space had a 9th one of these that didn't really work out very well. Maybe they'll finally get it right on the tenth one.

Pod people - The name given to the group of aliens who appear in *Invasion of the Body Snatchers* (1956) and its various remakes. A Pod Person is a perfect replica of its host (although completely emotionless, which pretty much gives the game away). The process begins with the alien lifeforms in a spore-like form that invade the planet Earth; they then select a human, create a duplicate of it (disintegrating the original human) and sulkily mope around eating all our food and using all our stuff. The whole thing is supposed to be a thinly veiled commentary on communism, in case you didn't know.

Poltergeist - A type of ghost that makes a lot of noise and throws stuff around. The word comes from the two German words "poltern" (to make sounds) and "geist" (ghost).

Potter's Bluff - A clean, picturesque New England coastal town filled with old fashioned friendliness and brutal murders. Features in *Dead & Buried* (1981).

Pornographic horror film - A subgenre that speaks for itself, really. Some of the more comical titles include: *The Human Sexipede, The XXXorcist, Evil Head, A Wet Dream on Elm Street, Re-Penetrator* and *The Texas Vibrator Massacre*.

POV (point-of-view) - A cinematic filming style for allowing the audience to see what a particular character is seeing. It is used predominately in slasher movies to show the audience who the killer is stalking. One of its most famous uses in horror movies is in John Carpenter's *Halloween*, which begins with a lengthy POV shot of a young Michael Myers spying on his sister before following her up the stairs to murder her. The 2012 remake of *Maniac* was shot almost entirely from the POV of its killer, Frank Zito (played by Elijah Wood). It was also a filming device used quite frequently by *Psycho* director Alfred Hitchcock.

Precious - The name of Buffalo Bill's dog in *The Silence of the Lambs*, proving that even violent and sadistic serial killers have a cute and cuddly side.

Predalien - A hybrid of a Xenomorph from the *Alien* franchise and a Predator from the *Predator* franchise, featured briefly in *Alien vs. Predator* (2004) and more frequently in the sequel *Alien vs. Predator: Requiem* (2007). It was the result of a facehugger impregnating a Predator. Clearly the production meeting to come up with the name was rather brief.

Predators - The name given to the ugly, hunting-fan species of aliens featured in the *Predator* film franchise. Predators are relentless and exceptional hunters who enjoy hunting us humans (and other alien species too) for sport. Their advanced alien technology assists them in the pursuit of their prey, and they revel in keeping grisly trophies from their successful kills (skins and skulls, for example). Top tip: To evade being spotted by the expert hunters with their highly advanced, superior technology, slap a bit of mud over your face.

Progeny - The offspring of humans, animals, plants… or aliens.

Prom (promenade dance) - A usually jovial celebration typically held at the end of the last year in high school. In horror movies, proms don't usually go so well and often end up in a total bloodbath. Notable examples: *Prom Night*, *Carrie* and *Cabin Fever 2: Spring Fever.*

Prosthetic makeup - The term given to the special effects makeup process involving sculpting, molding and casting to create various human and monster effects.

Psycho house - The name given to the large and rather spooky-looking house at the top of a small hill next to the Bates Motel in the *Psycho* movies. Norman Bates lives there with his dead mother. And lots of other dead things.

Psychokinesis - A type of mind power in which objects can be moved, manipulated or influenced by dramatically staring at them.

Psychopath - An unstable, aggressive, violent and mentally ill person who lacks empathy or remorse. Horror movies are peppered with them.

Pumpkin - A large, round, orangey fruit that people hollow out and carve faces into to celebrate Halloween. Often a candle or another light-source is placed inside, which is known as a jack-o'-lantern.

Pumpkinhead - A monstrous demon who lives in a pumpkin patch (obviously) featured in the *Pumpkinhead* horror film series. In the first movie, directed by special effects artist Stan Winston, the monster is summoned by a witch named Haggis, at the bequest of Ed Harley (Lance Henriksen), whose son was killed by some annoying teenagers. The resulting creature, a demon of vengeance, goes on a killing-spree, which is experienced via visions by Ed – as this is the price of seeking revenge. Things don't end too well, but Pumpkinhead popped out of the patch for three more sequels: *Blood Wings*, *Ashes to Ashes* and *Blood Feud*.

Purge – A really fun twelve-hour period when anyone is allowed to do whatever the hell they like. Murder tends to be at the top of everyone's list.

Pyramid - A mummy's home – usually located in Egypt, although similar structures are found all over the world. It is most likely that aliens built them.

Pyrokinesis - The alleged ability to be able to create and control fire with the power of the mind. The word was supposedly coined by Stephen King in his 1980 novel *Firestarter*.

Q

Q - The name of a winged serpent that lives in the Chrysler Building in New York City. Its full name is Quetzalcoatl – but just call it Q because that's all you'll have time to say before it tears you apart (according to the poster).

Quarantine – An attempt to confine something to restrict the spread of infections or viruses or alien entities. It never works in a horror film.

Quatermass, Bernard – A man who started out as a surveyor who then moved on to shooting people into space in rockets. He wasn't so keen on the results of his experiments, which saw people getting killed and aliens becoming involved, so he pretty much wished he'd stuck to surveying.

Quietness - A skill required should the world become overrun with aliens with an acute sense of hearing. It is highly recommended to shush people every five minutes to increase your chances of survival. Features in *A Quiet Place* (2018).

R

Rage - A fictional bloodborne virus featured in *28 Days Later* (2002) and *28 Weeks Later* (2007) that sends the host into an uncontrollable rage. But it doesn't, I repeat, *doesn't* turn them into a zombie.

Rats - A type of rodent commonly found in horror movies, because we're all a bit afraid of them. Notable rat appearances: *Willard* (1971/2003), *Deadly Eyes* (1982), *Rats: Night of Terror* (1984) and *Graveyard Shift* (1990).

Raven - A type of bird that is often associated with horror movies, possibly because they look a little spooky and they eat the flesh of dead animals. They have a long cultural history of being symbolic of death and evil.

Rawhead Rex - An ancient demon in Ireland who is unleased after a farmer wants a bit more room in his field by digging up a stone pillar. The monstrous-looking, toothy humanoid beast makes the best use of its newfound freedom by killing everyone it encounters. The creature was depicted as more of a giant penis in Clive Barker's original short story, but that might have been a bit weird in a horror movie.

Ray, Charles Lee - The name of the Lakeshore Strangler who went on to possess a Good Guy doll via a voodoo spell and was hence known as Chucky. Features in the *Child Play* movies – but not the 2019 remake.

Razorback - A colloquial name given to a crazy, giant wild boar. Features in the 1984 Australian film, *Razorback*.

Reagent - A luminously bright green liquid used for re-animating dead people… and cats. It also works on individual body parts – heads can be quite fun to re-animate autonomously. It can also be injected into separate body parts to create a Frankenstein's monster-esque new lifeform.

Reboot - The term horror filmmakers use when they don't want to admit they've basically remade the original film.

Redrum - Murder spelled backwards. In *The Shining*, Jack Torrance's son, Danny, repeatedly said it in a really creepy way before etching it onto a door with a lipstick. His parents didn't see the funny side.

Remake - A newly produced feature film based on specific characters, story elements and locations from a previously financially or critically successful film. Though not exclusive to the horror genre, remakes are quite widespread in the genre. They can be rather polarizing to fans, with some people (supposedly) refusing to even watch a remake of a classic horror film. They're rarely as good as the original film but some have proved more financially successful and even gone on to spawn their own sequels or prequels and, in some cases, remakes of remakes.

Repossessed - A term used when a person (let's call her Linda Blair) gets possessed by a demon once again, though in a more comical way this time.

Return - To either go to or come back from a particular place, or person. "Return" is a common word used in horror movie titles (often, but not always, in sequels). Horror film examples: *The Return of the Living Dead* (1985), *Return to Horror High* (1987), *Halloween 4: The Return of Michael Myers* (1988), *The Return of Swamp Thing* (1989) and *Return to House on Haunted Hill* (2007).

Revenant - Something that returns after a long absence, usually from the dead. The word is derivative of the French word meaning "returning." In folklore, a revenant can be a ghost or an animated corpse. The word is used in the title of the 2009 zombie horror film *The Revenant*.

Reverse-beartrap - A sadistic device that is attached to the head of someone who has been very naughty for the purposes of playing a fun little game. The contraption is locked with a padlock that the player has to locate a key to, which will be kept in some sort of grisly place (like inside someone's stomach, for example). If the padlock is not removed in a set amount of time the reverse-beartrap will open up and rip the jaws apart of the player. It's not really much fun. I prefer Monopoly.

Rheodsaurus - The name of the dinosaur-like monster featured in *The Beast from 20,000 Fathoms* (1953). The Rheodsaurus is unleashed after an atomic bomb test in the Arctic Circle and leaves a trail of destruction in its wake as it heads to New York City's Coney Island amusement park for some fun. Unfortunately, it's considered *waaaaay* too big for the rides, so the military kill it. Killjoys.

Rice - The vampire David from *The Lost Boys* can make you believe it's maggots. Party trick #2.

Ripley, Ellen - The archenemy of the alien species known as Xenomorphs. She really hates those things – one time she even called one a bitch. Despite her loathing for the creatures, she continued to return to fight them over the course of four *Alien* movies, even returning from the dead in *Alien: Resurrection* because she hadn't had quite enough Xenomorph extermination fun. She was portrayed by

Sigourney Weaver in all four movies.

Roadkill - A dead animal on the road, often seen at the beginning of a horror movie to let you know that bad things are about to happen.

Robert the Doll - A haunted doll owned by Florida-based painter and author Robert Eugene Otto that was the inspiration behind Chucky in the *Child's Play* movies. The doll features in the *Robert the Doll* film franchise by UK director Andrew Jones.

Rufus - The name of the cat belonging to Herbert West's housemate Dan Cain in *Re-Animator*. West (probably) killed it before bringing it back to life as a psychotic and ferocious undead beastie. In West's favor, he refrained from leaving a frank note declaring, "Cat dead, details later."

Ryder, John - The name of a hitchhiker that it is not advised you offer a ride to.

S

Sacrifyx - The name of the fictional thrash metal band featured in *The Gate* (1987) whose album, *The Dark Book*, contains lyrics that summon a horde of pint-sized demons from a hole in the backyard.

Salem - A city in Massachusetts, USA, which was the location of the Salem Witch Trials of 1692. On account of its horrific history it is often mentioned or featured in horror movies. Notable movies include: *The Covenant* (2006), *A Haunting in Salem* (2011), *The Lords of Salem* (2012) and *The Autopsy of Jane Doe* (2016).

Santa Carla - A Californian beach town also known as The Murder Capital of the World – they should really get a new slogan. If you can stomach all the damn vampires living there, it's a pretty picturesque place to live.

Santa Claus - A usually benevolent man who dresses in a red costume, sports a fluffy white beard and gives out presents to all the good children on Christmas Eve. In horror movies the same attire is usually worn by psychopaths who go around slaughtering everyone at Christmastime… good *or* bad. Notable examples: *Christmas Evil* (1980), *Silent Night, Deadly Night* (1984) and *Santa's Slay* (2005).

Satan - Another name for the Devil, the personification of evil. Despite his penchant for horror, Satan himself only intermittently shows his ugly face to us in the horror genre.

Satanism - A word that is commonly associated with devil-worship and evil, usually also involving ritualistic animal or human sacrifice. In reality it is a rather harmless religion promoting pride, liberty and individualism.

Sawyer, Drayton - An elderly cook from Texas who also owns a gas station. He doesn't really take pleasure in killing, like the rest of his family, but he sure loves cooking human meat, and never skimps on it in his award-winning chilies. He was portrayed by Jim Siedow in the first two *Texas Chainsaw Massacre* movies.

Scanners - A person with the ability to blow your head up by making lots of unusual facial gestures. Features in *Scanners* (1981), *Scanners II: The New Order* and *Scanners III: The Takeover* (1992) and the spin-offs *Scanner Cop* (1994) and *Scanner Cop II* (1995).

Scarecrow - A human-shaped and life-sized figure mainly used in farming to stop birds from eating seeds and crops. It wasn't until the early 80s that scarecrows first cropped up (pun intended) in the horror genre. With something so creepy-looking, and with the word "scare" in its name, it's surprising it wasn't earlier. The first movie generally considered to be the first "Killer Scarecrow" movie is the 1981 TV movie *Dark Night of the Scarecrow*, which is now hailed as something of a classic in the horror genre. The other early notable title is the imaginatively titled 1988 film *Scarecrows*, which saw a bunch of bank robbers being stalked and killed by scarecrows when they landed their plane near to an abandoned farmhouse.

Scary movie - A more informal term for a horror film. Used in a sentence: "What's your favorite scary movie?"

Scooby-doo - A children's animated TV series that acts as the gateway show to a future love of horror movies for most horror fans. And we still love it. Well, I do anyway.

Schrecken - The German word for "scare," and also an alternative title for F. W. Murnau's 1920 lost horror movie, *The Head of Janus*. It's also the name of a short horror movie in *2 Die For* (2018), directed by Killian H. Gore. Me!

Scream Queen - The name given to an actress who has appeared in a number of horror movies, or has made a one-off appearance in a particularly notable horror movie. The term is derivative of "Screen Queen." Scream Queens tend not to be killed in a horror movie, it is more typical that they are the "Final Girl" or heroine who defeats the villain – although this isn't always the case. Some of the most well-known Scream Queens include Linda Blair, Danielle Harris, Marilyn Burns, Heather Langenkamp, Barbara Steele and, perhaps the Queen of the Scream Queens, Jamie Lee Curtis.

Screaming - A sound frequently made by people (usually female) in horror movies. The noise is often emitted when a character is frightened by something or being killed by someone or something.

Sea monster - An aquatic, monstrous creature living in the depths of the ocean that is somehow awakened, disturbed or unleashed by us clumsy humans. Sea monsters come in a variety of forms and may either be prehistoric, extraterrestrial, mutations (caused by humans) or genetically modified beasties. Horror movie appearances include: *Deep Rising* (1998), *Leviathan* (1989), *DeepStar Six* (1989) and *The Meg* (2018).

Séance - A meeting of a group of people (usually around a really nice table) in which contact with the dead is attempted. One of the group members tends to be a medium who will conduct the séance - they'll be the one really hamming-it-up in the scene. The word is derived from the French word meaning "session."

Sematary - Alternative spelling of "cemetery" from the Stephen King film adaptation *Pet Sematary*. It was King's intention to spell the word incorrectly to suggest that children had misspelled it. It isn't because Stephen King can't spell.

Sentinel Sphere - A flying metallic, silver (sometimes gold) ball featured throughout the five *Phantasm* movies. Although they resemble a completely benevolent Christmas ornament, Sentinel Spheres are deadly weapons used by The Tall Man and they house all sorts of deadly weapons like blades, drills and lasers. Inside each sphere is a human brain, which The Tall Man has placed inside so they look a bit more gruesome when they're opened.

Sequel - A continuation of either/all characters, story and location in a new movie, not distinct to the horror genre but, arguably, rather synonymous with it, particularly with slasher movies. Often it is only the antagonist (or antagonists) from the first film who appear in the sequel, with a new set of secondary characters and lead role/s, often, but not always, in the same general or specific location - for example: the *Friday the 13th*, *A Nightmare on Elm Street* and the *Hellraiser* movies. Other times the hero or heroine's story is continued alongside the antagonists such as in the *Scream* film series or, in a rather fragmented way, the *Halloween* movies. Some horror movies, such as the *Phantasm* franchise, more directly continue the story with the same characters in the sequels. Other sequels have a completely different story and set of characters and locations – such as *Dawn of the Dead*, *House 2: The Second Story* and *Halloween III: Season of the Witch* but keep similar themes from the original movie. The horror movie series with the most direct sequels is *Witchcraft* (1988), which has, to date, fifteen sequels.

Serial killer - A term used for someone who kills three or more people on separate occasions. Psychological or sexual gratification are usually their motivation and they often have a very particular choice of victim and a similar method (modus operandi) of carrying out their sadistic crimes. A lot of American serial killers have an almost celebrity-like status, which, in part, has been heightened by media portrayals of them. Ted Bundy, Jeffrey Dahmer and John Wayne Gacy are amongst America's most notorious and infamous serial killers. Notable horror films include: *Henry Portrait of a Serial Killer* (1986), *The Silence of the Lambs* (1991), *Se7en* (1995) and *Creep* (2014).

Se7en - Alternative spelling of "seven," referencing the seven deadly sins that serial killer John Doe used as a template to kill, you've guessed it, seven people he considered sinners.

Seven Doors Hotel - A hotel in Louisiana, USA, which houses one of the Seven Doors of Death in Room 36. Probably best to stay in room 1 or 2, just to be on the safe side. Features in *The Beyond* (1981).

Sex - The act of physical sexual activity. In slasher films, it usually leads to the deaths of the characters who perform sexual acts – likely because the film's antagonist isn't keen on such behavior. It is also featured in an abundant amount of horror movies merely to increase the box office takings. On rare occasions, sex can transmit unusual diseases which trigger random strangers to relentless follow you around.

Shaky-cam - The name given by the filmmakers of *The Evil Dead* to describe their makeshift Steadicam, used to simulate the evil entity running through the woods. Basically, they bolted the film camera to a chunk of wood and had two crewmembers hold either side of it as they ran. Simple, but effective. And very cheap.

Shape, The - An alternative name for Michael Myers in the *Halloween* motion picture franchise. Portrayed by Nick Castle in the original 1978 movie – a role he reprised (in part) in *Halloween* (2018). The origin of the word came from the description of Michael Myers in John Carpenter and Debra Hill's screenplay for *Halloween* in which they describe him as merely being a shape, lurking in the shadows.

Shark - A type of fish that likes to attack and kill humans (and sometimes dogs). In real-life, shark attacks on people are incredibly rare, although in horror movies they are rampant. The great white shark is perhaps the most common shark to swim across the silver screen, its popularity as a movie monster heightened by Steven Spielberg's *Jaws* in 1975. Some of the other notable great white shark movies include *The Reef* (2010), *Bait 3D* (2012), *47 Meters Down* (2017) and *The Shallows* (2016), and of course the three sequels to *Jaws*.

Shark cage - Or anti-shark cage – a "protective" cage used for observing dangerous sharks at close proximity. If you're using one in a horror movie it's most likely to be violently attacked by a great white shark and sink to the bottom of the ocean. Chances of survival are pretty low.

Sharknado - A tornado riddled with ravenous sharks, and not as rare as one might think. To date there have been six documented cases of sharknados across the world.

Sheep Zombie - Though quite rare, sometimes sheep can succumb to zombie-like symptoms if exposed to a virus that turns them into blood-thirsty man-eaters. There's only one notable documented case, chronicled in the 2006 New Zealand movie, *Black Sheep*.

Sheet - A ghost's number one choice of clothing.

Shining - A telepathic ability that allows someone to hear what other people are thinking, as well as communicate with other people from long distances and look into both the past and future. Quite a handy skill unless you find yourself snowed-in with an unstable father in a secluded hotel with a grisly past.

Shortcut - The name of an off-road, shorter, route to a particular location. It is not advised that you take one in a horror movie. Just go the long way around.

Shower - A place for cleaning oneself where you are also likely to be stabbed to death, especially in an off-the-beaten-track motel.

Shrooms - A type of hallucinogenic mushroom. Not a wise idea to take them in Irish woodlands. Feature in the 2007 movie *Shrooms*.

Sil - The name given to the human/alien hybrid featured in *Species* (1995). Her name is derived from the code name S1L, which was given to her in the laboratory where she was created from an extra-terrestrial message regarding DNA meddling. Clearly none of the scientists had ever watched an alien invasion movie and so they went ahead and used the alien DNA sequence and mixed it with human DNA. Bad idea.

Silent Hill - An abandoned, spooky town that, in another dimension, exists as a place inhabited by inhuman monsters. One of them has a giant pyramid on his head!

Silver bullet - The most surefire way to kill a werewolf is with a silver bullet. Yes, they may be expensive but it's worth the investment. Other items made of silver can also be effective in slaying a werewolf. It is commonly thought that the origin of the silver bullet's werewolf termination abilities comes from Jean Chastel, who killed the Beast of Gévaudan in France in 1767.

Silver Shamrock - The name of the evil organization featured in *Halloween III: Season of the Witch*. Silver Shamrock Novelties produce three Halloween masks (a Jack-o'-lantern, a witch and a skull) that are fitted with fragments of a rock stolen from Stonehenge inside a microchip hidden within the mask. A catchy tune on a TV advert counts down the moment in which the masks will be activated and unpleasantly kill all those wearing them. Unfortunately, Tom Atkins does a pretty bad job of trying to thwart Silver Shamrock's plans.

Six-six-six (666) - The number of the beast. 666, according to the Book of Revelation, is the Devil's number (not his phone number). In horror movies it is perhaps best-known for being the symbol of the Antichrist in *The Omen* movies.

Sixth sense (AKA extrasensory perception or ESP) - The speculated psychic human sense for telepathy, clairvoyance and for seeing dead people and Bruce Willis.

Skeleton - The complete set of bones inside a human or animal. Being such a macabre image, skeletons often appear in horror films, and sometimes even come back to life.

Skinny dipping - The practice of swimming without any clothes on. In horror movies it is common to do this in bodies of water that are host to dangerous animals such as sharks or piranhas, or close by to locations where deranged killers are on the loose.

Skull - The skeletal head of a human or animal. Skulls are frequent visitors to the horror film and can even be a visual representation of the genre. Skull images feature on countless horror film posters and artwork.

Slasher film - A horror movie subgenre usually consisting of a deranged murderer killing teenagers in a variety of gory ways. Although the origins of the subgenre can be traced to the early days of cinema, it is most commonly agreed that *Halloween* (1978) began the slasher movie boom that continued till 1984 – the '78 – '84 boom is regarded as the Golden Age of the slasher movie with over 100 movies being produced in the six year period. In J. A. Kerswell's *The Teenage Slasher Movie Book*, Kerswell cites the following ten films as key examples of the subgenre: *Friday the 13th* (1980), *Prom Night* (1980), *Terror Train* (1980), *The Burning* (1981), *The Funhouse* (1981), *Happy Birthday to Me* (1981), *Hell Night* (1981), *My Bloody Valentine* (1981), *The House on Sorority Row* (1983) and *A Nightmare on Elm Street* (1984).

Slaughtered Lamb - A public house in the Yorkshire moors where the locals are likely to completely stop what they are doing and stare at you when you walk through the door.

Slaughterhouse - A building in which animals are killed for the purposes of providing meat for human consumption. For Leatherface and his family in *The Texas Chain Saw Massacre*, they're more of a place to have a fun-filled family day out. The rather brutal imagery of a slaughterhouse is often referenced or featured in horror movies, though its more notable appearance is probably in the 1987 slasher movie, *Slaughterhouse*.

Sleepy Hollow - The name of a village in New York that is the setting for author Washington Irving's short story *The Legend of Sleepy Hollow* – home to a headless horseman and lots of other spooky delights.

Slender Man - The name of a viral Creepypasta created by Eric Knudsen in 2009 after a contest was launched on the Something Awful internet forum to make the best paranormal image. The Slender Man is depicted as a tall, thin, featureless man in a black suit and described as a character who abducts and kills children. To date, the Slender Man has made two horror movie appearances, firstly in *Always Watching: A Marble Hornets Story* (where he is known as The Operator) (2015) and more recently in *Slender Man* (2018).

Slugs - They slime, they ooze, they kill - but only really in the 1988 horror movie, *Slugs*, based on Shaun Hutson's book. Aside from that, they pretty much just quietly slither about on the ground and keep to themselves.

Smiths Grove Sanitarium - The name of the mental institution in

Illinois where a young Michael Myers was detained after killing his older sister on Halloween night in 1963. Considering the deranged and violent inmates, the security is rather lax.

Snake - A long, slithering reptile with no legs, big jaws, considerable squashing skills and an intrinsic capability to send a collective shiver down the spines of most human beings. Some of them also administer venom to us, whether we want it or not (usually, not). Snakes are responsible for over 100,000 deaths a year, so are a pretty prolific killer – definitely not a creature to trifle with.

Snuff films - A horror film that purports to feature scenes of people being killed for real. Though it's possible (and likely) that such films exist, they were viewed as more of an urban legend back in the seventies, which the low-budget indie distributor Allan Shackleton cashed-in on by releasing a film (originally named *Slaughter*) he owned with a newly filmed ending, supposedly showing an actual murder. He renamed it *Snuff* and promoted it as an actual snuff film, featuring the tagline, "The film that could only be made in South American… where life is cheap!" Of course, the murder was staged, and everybody had a good laugh about it later.

Solyent Green - It's people! It's made out of people!

Sororicide - The act of someone killing their own sister. Notable horror movie example: *Halloween* (1978).

Soul - Something coveted by demonic characters. I've no idea why they seem to like them so much. Although I imagine they taste pretty good with chips.

Space - That huge area above our heads full of stars and planets. It is also the location where some horror film franchises have chosen to (often inexplicably) set their latest installment, presumably when they've run out of ideas. Notable horror movies include: *Jason X* (2002), *Hellraiser: Bloodline* (1996), *Critters 4* (1992) and *Leprechaun 4: In Space* (1996).

Space Jockey - A nickname for the mysterious alien creature that was seen sitting in some kind of chair in a derelict spacecraft in *Alien*

(1979). Turns out it was an Engineer whose kind created the human race back in the day. Who would have thought?

Special effects makeup (or SFX) - An umbrella term for the various methods of creating the blood, gore, makeups and monsters that feature predominantly in horror films. Unlike in many other film genres, the special effects artists often receive a credit in the opening titles in horror films and many have become celebrities themselves for their wonderfully gruesome creations. Some notable horror movie special effects makeup artists include: Tom Savini (*Dawn of the Dead*), Stan Winston (Aliens), Dick Smith (*The Exorcist*), Rick Baker (*An American Werewolf in London*) Rob Bottin (*The Thing*) and Mark Shostrom (*Evil Dead II*).

Spengler, Lori - The name of the killer who sports a creepy babyface mask in the 2017 slasher movie *Happy Death Day* (and *Happy Death Day 2U*). I probably should have preceded that sentence with "spoiler alert," sorry. On account of a *Groundhog Day*-esque time loop, Spengler both does and doesn't kill the film's protagonist, Theresa Gelbman, multiple times throughout the film. So maybe she's not really a killer at all. But she kind of is. I think. Things get more confusing in *Happy Death Day 2U*.

Spider - An eight-legged creature that is known as one of the hardest working prop-makers in the horror movie industry. Spiders also make an excellent horror movie monster, as they scare the pants off the majority of people (don't try to be all tough and deny it).

Splatter films - A horror movie subgenre featuring an abundance of gore and violence. Herschell Gordon Lewis' *Blood Feast* (1963) is often cited as the first splatter film. The term was coined by George A. Romero in reference to his own movie, *Dawn of the Dead*.

Springwood - A fictional town in Ohio that is the main setting for the *A Nightmare on Elm Street* movies. Best avoided by children and teenagers.

Springwood Slasher - An alternative name for Freddy Krueger from the *A Nightmare on Elm Street* movies. More commonly associated with Krueger's character whilst he was still a living serial killer, and not bothering youngsters in their dreams.

Squib - A small explosive device that is used in films to simulate a bullet hit on a person's body. Usually it is placed behind a bag containing fake blood so that it looks more realistic when staging a bullet hit.

Stab film series - The *Stab* films feature within the *Scream* movie franchise and aren't real horror movies themselves, though some scenes do appear in the *Scream* movies, and *Scream 3* is centered around the production of *Stab 3*. The *Stab* films consist of: *Stab*, *Stab 2*, *Stab 3: Return to Woodsboro* (renamed to *Hollywood Horror* after the events of *Scream 3*), *Stab 4: Knife of Doom*, *Stab 5: Clock of Doom*, *Stab 6: Ghostface Returns* and *Stab 7*. According to the character Jenny Randall in *Scream 4*, *Stab 5* is the worst *Stab* movie as it featured time travel.

Stab - The action of thrusting a weapon into a victim. Mostly associated with knives.

Stake - A wooden, pointed implement that is used for killing vampires when driven into their hearts. Various types of wood are considered more effective including ash, hawthorn, oak and aspen.

Stoner - The name of a character who frequently smokes marijuana. Bad shit tends to happen to them in horror movies.

Stripe - The main Gremlin creature featured in the first *Gremlins* movie. Stripe is the leader of the pack and the main antagonist of both Billy and Gizmo. His name derives from the tuft of white hair atop his head. Although he seems smarter and more devious than the rest of his clan, his evil plans for world domination are thwarted when Gizmo opens the blinds.

Strip Monopoly - A fun variation of the popular board game Monopoly that is sometimes played at summer camps to pass the time before being slaughtered.

Stuff, The - A delicious-looking and tasting, yogurt/ice-cream white-colored substance, which is actually calorie-free! What's the catch? Well, aside from being highly addictive, it's made from a living organism that will ultimately destroy your mind and body, turning you into a zombie and melting your face off. Features in *The Stuff* (1985).

Sumatran Rat-monkey - A hybrid species of a monkey and a rat that originates from Skull Island (King Kong's home). The creature is the result of tree monkeys being raped by giant plague-bearing rats – the Sumatran Rat-monkey offspring are host to the Rage Plague Virus, which turns anyone unfortunate enough to be bitten by one into a flesh-eating zombie. Features in *Braindead* (aka *Dead Alive*) (1992).

Summer camp - A place where youngsters go over the summer to play sports, swim, canoe, engage in other fun or academic activities and tell scary stories around the campfire. In America there is a high probability that the local urban legend will come to life and kill you.

Summerisle - The name of the remote Hebridean island where the jovial locals enjoy partaking in a whole host of fun activities including drinking, singing, dancing, dressing-up, and, of course, human sacrifice.

Sunglasses - A form of eyewear used to protect the eyes from the sun, or just to look cool. On one occasion a guy named Ray Nelson put on a pair and could see the world for what it really was – namely, overrun by aliens and littered with messages to tell everyone to "Obey," "Conform," "Consume," "Watch TV," and "Buy Killian H. Gore's books." Features in John Carpenter's *They Live* (1988).

Suspiria - The word used as the title for Dario Argento's classic 1977 film is derived from the Latin phrase, "Suspiria de profundis," which translates to, "Sighs from the depths." So that clears that up.

T

Tall Man - The Tall Man is the main antagonist in the *Phantasm* film franchise, portrayed by Angus Scrimm in all five movies. He doesn't say an awful lot, but when he does speak it's usually in a rather menacing tone and said with a grimace. Obviously, he's rather tall, white haired and always wears a suit and a raised eyebrow. He hails from a planet known only as The Red Planet, but it's not Mars, and before becoming an incredibly looming mortician at Morningside mortuary he was known as Jebediah Morningside and messed around with interdimensional travel in his spare time. The Tall Man is a very powerful villain, although he's not so keen on ice. Or ice cream vendors, for that matter.

Tarker's Mill – A lovely little Maine town – but make sure you bring some silver bullets if you're visiting. Shares a border with Chester's Mill – that town under the massive dome. Probably best just avoiding anywhere with the word "Mill" in the name if you're in that area.

Tarman - The name given to the gooey, flimsy-moving zombie in *The Return of the Living Dead* (1985). Tarman was originally located in the cannister that the characters Frank and Freddy unwittingly opened, unleashing the noxious, reanimating gas Trioxin 245. As well as appearing in the first movie, Tarman appeared in the 1988 sequel, *Return of the Living Dead II*, again played by actor Allan Trautman – he also appears briefly in *Return of the Living Dead: Rave to the Grave* (2005), played by a different actor. Tarman's hobbies include hiding in basements and eating brains.

Taxidermy - The favorite pastime (murder aside) of Norman Bates in the *Psycho* movies. Taxidermy animals can be found fairly frequently in horror films, probably because they're inanimate dead animals desperate to give us all a fright by coming back to life (which one of them famously did in *Evil Dead II*). Other notable appearances include: *Night of the Living Dead* (1968), *The Lost Boys* (1987) and *The Cabin in the Woods* (2012).

Taylor, Mick - The killer from the Australian outback who features in the *Wolf Creek* movies and TV show. He's a jovial bloke with a quirky chuckle, but don't let that fool you, as Mick is a cold-hearted, sadistic psychopath who sees killing as more of a sport. He doesn't like backpackers, or anyone else for that matter. Mick's hobbies include hunting, torture (psychological and physical), murder, rape and meeting new people.

Tears - A waste of good suffering.

Telepod - A teleportation device that is useful for transporting people (but not always baboons) from one side of the room to the other. The inventor, Seth Brundle, gets a bit tipsy one night and accidentally takes a fly in with him. It results in something he jovially refers to as a Brundlefly (a name he clearly thought long and hard about).

Thing, The - An alien being featured in the three *The Thing* movies. The original 1951 movie aside, The Thing is an alien creature that can mimic the form of any organism it chooses. Given half the chance it will wipe out the entire world population in 27,000 hours — which is about three years. In *The Thing from Another World*, it was portrayed as a Frankenstein-like humanoid that most people said resembled a carrot. It is not known how many years that version of The Thing would have turned the world's population into carrots.

Thirteen (13) - A number used quite frequently in horror movies as it is synonymous with bad luck. The numbers in Stephen King's short story and film adaptation, *1408* (2007), add up to 13. The number can often be used in horror movies as the amount of victims or a span of years, or a room number or house address, or feature in some other way to add a dash of spookiness.

Thorn, Damien - The name of the character in *The Omen* films who is the son of a jackal and someone named Satan. He was born on the sixth of June at 6 o'clock in the morning (which everyone should have been a bit more freaked out about, really) and was adopted by an American ambassador and his wife in the UK. Aside from the occasional nanny suicide, impalement and decapitation, it was a pretty ordinary childhood. Damien is eventually discovered to be the antichrist - the 666 birthmark on his head was a bit of a giveaway.

Three-D (3D) - A photographic and screening technique which creates an added depth to a motion picture, making it more three-dimensional. In the 50s it become popular in the horror genre with films such as *House of Wax* (1953), *It Came from Outer Space* (1953), *House on Haunted Hill* (1959) and *Creature from the Black Lagoon* (1954). There was a brief resurgence of 3D horror movies in the early 80s, most notably with the movies *Friday the 13th Part 3: 3D* (1982), *Jaws 3-D* (1983) and *Amityville 3-D* (1983).

Thunder and lightning - The most common type of weather in a horror movie. If you want to be scientific about it, thunder is actually the sound caused by lightning. In horror movies thunder and lightning is often a lot more exaggerated than it is in real life and tends to occur a lot more frequently too. In the movie *Poltergeist*, we all learned that counting after a flash of lighting until a clap of thunder informs us how near or far the storm is from us.

Timberline Lodge - The name of the mountainside hotel that was used as the exterior of the Overlook Hotel in *The Shining* (1980). Located on the south side of Mount Hood in Clackamas County, Oregon.

Titty Twister - The name of the desert-based strip club featured in *From Dusk Till Dawn* (1996). Alongside the usual range of wines, beers, cocktails and spirits there's also a wide variety of "pussy" available.

Todd, Sweeney - A fictional character and urban legend also known as The Demon Barber of Fleet Street. The original version of the story involves Todd killing people in his barber's shop by dropping them through a trapdoor into his basement (where he slits their throats with a cut-throat razor, if they're not already dead) and disposing of their bodies by cutting them up to be served as meat pies in Mrs. Lovett's (his partner in crime) pie shop. The character first appeared in film in the lost 1926 film *Sweeney Todd*, although it is Tod Slaughter's portrayal of the character that is perhaps most well known in the 1936 film *Sweeney Todd: The Demon Barber of Fleet Street*, as well as Johnny Depp's portrayal in Tim Burton's 2007 musical adaptation of the story.

Tomato - A round, red fruit usually eaten or drunk (or thrown at people) all over the world. Not hugely occurrent as an antagonist in horror movies aside from the 70's horror movie *Attack of the Killer Tomatoes*. Those same killer tomatoes returned for more killing in 1988, struck again in 1990 and ate France in 1991. They've returned to being food since then.

Torture porn - An informal term for a subgenre of horror movie featuring sadistic and gratuitous violence. The theme of human torturing is more often than not central to the story itself. The *Saw* and *Hostel* film franchises are perhaps the most well-known torture porn movies.

Torrance, Jack - The name of the character in *The Shining* who, along with his family, looked after a secluded hotel for the winter. Jack spent the majority of his time working on an untitled novel, which mostly consisted of the words, "All work and no play makes Jack a dull boy." He did change-up the spacing of those words to make it a bit more interesting, though.

Toulon, André - The name of the French puppeteer in the *Puppet Master* film franchise who is responsible for the creation of the various deadly puppets featured in the film series.

Toxic Avenger, The - The name of the superhero-like ex-janitor featured in *The Toxic Avenger* film series. He started out as a frail and nerdy man named Melvin who was chased by some bullies until he fell into a barrel of toxic waste. Rather than end up dead (which I'm pretty sure would happen in real life) Melvin was transformed into a badly disfigured monster with inhuman strength.

Transylvania - The region in Romania that is heavily associated with Count Dracula on account of Bram Stoker's seminal 1897 novel, *Dracula,* which was partially set there. Aside from Dracula, the area is also more generally associated with vampires and other supernatural phenomena.

Triffid - A species of monstrous alien plant that can also move (very slowly) and lethally sting people. In John Wyndham's *Day of the Triffids* book, the triffids were not extraterrestrial in origin, or at least it was never chronicled as such – it was hinted at that they were bioengineered.

Trioxin 245 - A gas-liquid featured in *The Return of the Living Dead* that is initially encased in cannisters kept safely in the basement of the Uneeda Medical Supply building. Unfortunately, in gloating about the cannisters they are accidentally breached by one of the employees, unleashing the reanimating gasses onto the nearby graveyard. Naturally, total chaos and lots of brain-eating ensued.

Trixie - Despite its rather playful sounding name, the rabies-like Trixie virus was spread through the tainted water supply in George Romero country in the seventies and 2010. It causes people to become "crazies," exhibiting strange and malevolent behavior.

Troll - An ugly, rather dim, humanoid creature from Norse mythology and Scandinavian folklore that can come in a variety of sizes. Trolls tend to live in isolated areas in the mountains or caves and can be very hostile to human beings. Exposure to sunlight can have the ability to turn them into stone. Notable horror movies: *Trollhunter* (2010), *The Gate* (1987), *Cat's Eye* (1985), *Troll* (1986), but *not Troll 2* (because they're goblins).

Troma Entertainment - An independent US film production and distribution company founded in 1974 by Lloyd Kaufman and Michael Herz in New York City. Troma films are low budget B-movies, known for being particularly shocking, gory, excessively violent and featuring gratuitous nudity. They're also very funny. The many movies Troma have both produced and distributed often have big cult followings. Some of Troma's more notable titles include: *The Toxic Avenger* (1984), *Class of Nuke 'Em High* (1986), *Poultrygeist: Night of the Chicken Dead* (2006), *Surf Nazis Must Die* (1987), *Rabid Grannies* (1988), *A Nymphoid Barbarian in Dinosaur Hell* (1990) and *Monster in the Closet* (1986).

Tromaville - The name of the fictional New Jersey location where many of the films made by Troma Entertainment are set.

True Knot – A gang of vampire-like psychics who consume the "steam" emitted from children who have the ability to "shine." It keeps the members of the tribe younger and is a lot cheaper than plastic surgery.

Tucker and Dale – The names of two friends who were just trying to do up their cabin in the woods when a series of unfortunate events led to them being mistaken for hillbilly killers. Much hilarity and bloodshed ensued.

Turn - Not advisable to make a wrong one – especially in West Virginia.

TV spin-off - A television series using a particular horror film, or film series, as its inspiration. In the 80s there was only really a couple of them – *Freddy's Nightmares* and *Friday the 13th: The Series*, but they have grown in popularity of late with spin-offs of *Psycho* (*Bates Motel*), *The Evil Dead* (*Ash vs Evil Dead*), *Scream*, *The Exorcist*, *From Dusk Till Dawn*, *The Silence of the Lambs* (*Hannibal*), *The Purge*, *The Omen* (*Damien*), *What We Do in the Shadows*, *Wolf Creek* and *Creepshow*.

Twilight - The name of a series of teen vampire movies that nobody in the horror community really likes.

Twilight Zone - A hypothesized fifth dimension – a dimension of sound, sight and mind that is both shadow and substance of things and ideas. You'll know you've crossed over into when weird things start happening to you.

Twinkie - A small, yellow sponge cake with a creamy filling that was highly sought after during a zombie apocalypse by a man known as Tallahassee. It's also a snack that Gill-man is quite keen on stealing from children.

Twins - Two offspring produced from the same pregnancy, often to be found in horror movies - although perhaps the most famous horror film twins aren't supposed to be twins at all. The Grady girls in *The Shining* (1980) are often referred to as twins, but in both Stephen King's novel and the 1980 film adaptation they are only supposed to be sisters. The hotel manager, Stuart Ullman, refers to them as being, "About eight and ten." The confusion likely stems from the fact that the Grady girls were portrayed by real-life twins Lisa and Louise Burns. And they confuse things further by referring to themselves on their social media as "The Shining Twins". Notable twin movies include: *Twins of Evil* (1971), *Dead Ringers* (1988), *Basket Case* (1982) and *Seconds Apart* (2011).

Twist ending - A surprise reveal at the end of a movie. Not exclusive to the horror genre, but owing to a horror movie's intention to shock, quite frequently used. *The Sixth Sense* director M. Night Shyamalan loves them.

U

Über Jason - The futuristic, upgraded cyborg version of Jason Voorhees featured towards the end of *Jason X* (2002).

Umbrella Corporation - The name of the fictional pharmaceutical organization in the *Resident Evil* movies, responsible for unleashing the T-virus, which turns people into zombies.

Uncle Orange - The code name used by the filmmakers whilst filming *Halloween* (2018) to ensure the locations weren't hounded by horror fans... they still were, though. That man in the white mask kinda gave the game away.

Uncut - A term used more in the UK that horror fans like to see on the front or back of a DVD or Blu-ray horror movie box. On account of the huge amount of scenes cut from classic horror films in the 80s and 90s (by that nasty bunch at the BBFC) it's reassuring to see this word to inform the viewer that they can finally view all the gory bits that they were once thought too mentally unstable to be able to cope with.

Undead - A term used to describe either vampires or zombies. The undead are technically no longer living but are reanimated by some type of supernatural occurrence.

Uneeda Medical Supply - A warehouse in Louisville, Kentucky, USA, filled with skeletons, split dogs, frozen cadavers and other various supplies for the medical industry. Just don't mess with those cannisters in the basement and you should be fine.

Universal Monsters (or Universal Classic Monsters) - The collective name given to the classic monster movies produced and released by Universal Studios in the 1920s through to the 1950s. The 1923 film, *The Hunchback of Notre Dame*, starring Lon Chaney, was the first film - although it was, arguably, the two 1931 films, *Dracula* and *Frankenstein* that gave birth to the true, and most celebrated, run of Universal Monster movies. The main monsters are Dracula,

Frankenstein, The Mummy, The Invisible Man, The Wolf Man and Gill-man (Creature from the Black Lagoon). All of the listed monsters went on to spawn multiple sequels and crossovers.

Unofficial sequel - To cash-in on the popularity of certain horror movies, some dubious distribution companies and filmmakers (usually from Italy) would produce a movie completely unrelated to a horror film franchise and label it as a sequel in order to capitalize on its success. Notable examples include: *Alien 2: On Earth* (1980), *Jaws 5: Cruel Jaws* (1995) *Troll 2* and *Zombi 2* (1979).

Unrated - A term used mostly in American for a film that has been submitted to the MPAA (Motion Picture Association of America), but cuts have been suggested by them in order for the film to reach a wider audience in movie theaters – the omitted footage is then reinstated for the film's home video release and referred to as the "Unrated" version.

Uxoricide - The act of murdering your wife. Notable horror movie example: *The Stepfather* (1987).

V

Valak - The name of a demon from *The Conjuring* film Universe. Valak's guise as a nun is perhaps the most prominent version of the demon, and the most iconic.

Valek, Jan - A 600-year-old vampire who started out as a Catholic priest in Prague before a thwarted attempt at an exorcism turned him into a vampire. He is the head vampire featured in John Carpenter's *Vampires* (1998) and portrayed by Thomas Ian Griffith. Sample dialogue: "You can't kill me." But a good-old flash of sunlight exposed by vampire hunter Jack Crow (James Woods) proved otherwise.

Valentine Bluffs - The name of the fictional mining town featured in *My Bloody Valentine* (1981). Avoid on Valentine's Day.

Valentine's Day - Usually a day reserved for love and romance. In horror movies it's a day for murder and violence. Notable horror movies include: *My Bloody Valentine* (1981/2009), *X-Ray* (1981), *Lover's Lane* (1999) and *Valentine* (2001).

Valentine, Tiffany - The name of the female doll in the *Child's Play* movies, voiced by actress Jennifer Tilly. Tiffany was the girlfriend of serial killer Charles Lee Ray, before he went all "dolly" on her. She ultimately ended up being transferred into a doll (by Chucky) herself in the 1998 film *Bride of Chucky*. She's every bit as vulgar and violent as her partner in crime, so they make quite the perfect couple.

Vampire - An undead person who feeds on the blood of the living in order to survive. Vampires are immortals who can only come out at night (as sunlight is deadly to them). In horror movies, vampires are one of the most predominant and famous movie monsters and have had many variations over the years. The 1896 Georges Méliès film *Le Manoir du Diable* (*The House of the Devil* aka *The Haunted Castle*) is often considered to be the first film to feature a vampire (although it's only 3 minutes long, so perhaps look it up on YouTube rather than buy the Blu-ray).

Vas-o-cam - The name given to a low-budget version of a dolly track, invented by Tim Philo and used on the 1981 film, *The Evil Dead*. Instead of purchasing costly tracking equipment, director Sam Raimi and co simply laid down some gaffer tape on a plank of wood and coated it with Vaseline – then slid the camera along it. Groovy!

Velocipastor - A cross between a velociraptor and a pastor. Seriously. They made a movie about this. I'm not even kidding!

Ventriloquist's dummy - A type of puppet operated by a comedy performer, who also provides the voice. Ventriloquist's dummies have appeared in a number of horror movies, usually having been possessed in some way to take on a life of their own. Notable examples include: *Magic* (1978), *Dead of Night* (1945), *Dead Silence* (2007) and, of course, Slappy the Dummy from *Goosebumps* (2015).

Vernon, Leslie - The central killer and subject of the mock-documentary in the 2006 comedy-horror movie *Behind the Mask: The Rise of Leslie Vernon*, portrayed by Nathan Baesel. Despite his overtly friendly persona, Leslie is actually a slasher movie killer who is quite open about his lifestyle choice and very casually discusses his upcoming killing spree as if he's merely talking about opening up a new restaurant.

Vestron Video - A video distribution and production company founded in 1981 by Austin Owen Furst and notable for being behind a string of cult 80's and 90's horror movies including *Chopping Mall* (1986), *Slaughter High* (1986), *Waxwork* (1988), *Parents* (1989), *The Gate* (1987), *Class of 1999* (1990) and *Wishmaster* (1997).

VHS (Video Home System) - The name for the magnetic tape format launched in 1976 that was re-recordable and predominately used in the video rental market popular in the eighties and nineties. Despite VHS tapes often getting chewed by the video player, the grainy image, the full-frame pan-and-scan transfer and the heavy censorship of the films (particularly in the UK), VHS tapes are now seeing a resurgence for reasons of nostalgia amongst horror fans.

Video store - An establishment filled with videotapes that were available to rent for a short period of time. They were hugely popular in the eighties and nineties and are still fondly remembered by horror fans to this day. For people who grew up during their heyday, they were the places where they first obtained the horror movies that they continue to love and cherish. Sadly, video stores aren't really around anymore and when you try to explain about them to youngsters, you're pretty much greeted with a rather blank expression.

Video Nasty - A term used in the UK to categorize the movies (usually horror) that were particularly violent, explicit and/or gory that were eventually banned by the BBFC (British Board of Film Classification). Initially, the films were released on video as there was a loophole in the classification laws, but an uppity lady named Mary Whitehouse took care of that and a new act was passed (Video Recordings Act 1984) that saw all our lovely uncensored horror movies being dragged away and stored at Mary's house. Some notable video nasties include *The Evil Dead* (1981), *The Last House on the Left* (1972), *The Beyond* (1981), *The Burning* (1981), *The Toolbox Murders* (1978) and *The Funhouse* (1981) plus a load of other titles that you can now buy totally uncut at your local supermarket.

Vincent, Peter - A fictional horror film actor and TV show host who is roped into helping kill real-life vampires in the *Fright Night* movies. He was portrayed by Roddy McDowall in the first two 80's *Fright Night* movies and David Tennant in the 2011 remake (his character changed to a magician, for some reason).

Vine - A plant with a slender stem that grows on the ground or climbs upwards. If found around a Mayan ruin it may have a bloodlust and an ability to mimic sounds to lure you to your death. Features in *The Ruins* (2008).

Vinyl record - A flat disc containing an audio recording (usually music). Makes a pretty good weapon when flung at a zombie.

Virgin - A person who has yet to engage in sexual intercourse with another person. Virgins are considered very safe in slasher movies, though.

Vlad the Impaler - The inspiration for Bram Stoker's *Dracula* novel. The real Vlad, whose actual name was Vlad III Dracula (or Dracul), was quite partial to impaling people on stakes and leaving them to die. He'd often sit around and eat his dinner nearby whilst they died, and even dipped his bread in blood collected in jars from the bodies. The alleged site of his burial was exhumed in the 1930s, but Vlad's remains were not inside. So, he probably was a real vampire after all, and he's still out there! *Argh!*

Voodoo - A religion that is usually portrayed as being rather supernatural and ominous in horror movies and often associated with rituals and scary curses. In reality it's more about magic and worshiping spirits with elements from the Catholic church. It's nothing to worry about... although it was Voodoo that brought Chucky to life.

Voodoo doll - An effigy into which pins are stuck into after casting a spell to bring harm to a selected person. We all tried it on our teddy bears when we were kids. Or was that just me?

Voorhees, Jason - The name of the main villain in the *Friday the 13th* film franchise and one of the most famous slasher movie killers in horror movie history. Jason drowned in Crystal Lake as a little boy...

or so we were led to believe. He actually survived and lived in the woods, exacting revenge on the camp counselors who chopped his mom's head off (you can understand why he's so annoyed). Jason was eventually killed by a kid who made horror masks just like Tom Savini's (which were made by Tom Savini) – who, some years later, accidentally brought him back to life when he was innocently trying to desecrate his corpse. If there's actually any logic to the *Friday the 13th* timeline, it was thrown out of the window in later films and Jason just seemed to keep coming back, again and again. But we all love him, so he's most welcome. Although he appears to have been missing from the big screen for quite some time on account of an ongoing legal better over the rights. Please sort it out!

Voorhees, Pamela - The mother of Jason Voorhees from the *Friday the 13th* movies. As we all know now (because of *Scream*), Mrs. Voorhees was the central killer in the first *Friday the 13th* film. Initially Pam was a cook at Camp Crystal Lake when her son ("His name was Jason") drowned in the lake. She blamed the camp counselors, who were making love when they should have been watching him. Rather than file a lawsuit for negligence, she returned to the camp to kill the two camp counselors (Barry and Claudette). Years later, clearly completely nuts by now, she came back again to kill a totally unrelated bunch of summer camp workers. To put an end to her killing spree, one of the counselors, Alice, chopped her head off. Of course, that was just the beginning of the troubles at Crystal Lake.

W

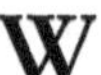

Walking dead - another term for a zombie, popularized by the TV show of the same name – which will probably be in its hundredth season by now. After much mystery over the origin of the zombie outbreak, creator Robert Kirkman was recently asked by a fan on Twitter what caused the zombies, to which he casually responded, "Space spore."

Walter, Diana - A malevolent ghost who can only appear when it's dark – this is on account of a rare skin condition she had in life whereby the slightest hint of light could cause her skin to burn. Best to keep the light on if she drops by. Features in the 2016 film *Lights Out.*

Warren, Ed and Lorraine - A man and wife paranormal investigation team who were the inspiration behind the two lead characters in *The Conjuring* movies. Amongst the many cases they worked on, they are perhaps best-known for their involvement in the Amityville investigations.

Water - A usually totally benevolent liquid for drinking, cooking, washing and irrigation. In horror films, malevolent creatures lurk in it. Movie aliens can have differing reactions to it – in *The Faculty* (1998), they need it to survive and in *Signs* (2002) it kills them. So, the jury is out on what we'd use water for in the case of a real-life alien invasion.

Waxwork - A lifelike type of dummy that has been created using wax. Along with other model forms (puppets, mannequins, dolls etc.) that resemble humans, waxworks are most welcome in the horror genre.

We Slaughter Barbeque - A friendly, family-run gas station in Texas. The barbeque is to-die-for. Sometimes referred to as Last Chance Gas.

Wednesday, see you next - A running-joke in the films of John Landis. Features in Landis' horror movies *An American Werewolf in London* (as the name of a porno film), *Twilight Zone: The Movie* (as a line of dialogue spoken in German), *Innocent Blood* (written on a marquee) and in Michael Jackson's *Thriller* video (spoken in the cinema and on the posters outside the theater). It originates from a line in Stanley Kubrick's *2001: A Space Odyssey* (1968).

Wendigo - A primal demon from Stephen King's *Pet Sematary* novel, responsible for cursing the Micmac burial ground. It is only hinted at in the 1989 film, though plays a much larger role in the 2019 remake.

Werewolf - The name of a shapeshifting creature that flirts between human and wolf-like beast. Typically, the transformation occurs to the person when there is a full moon. A werewolf has many forms but often they take the guise of a monstrous, large wolf or a more humanoid shape with various wolf attributes. Werewolves are one of the most common horror film monsters and have appeared in the genre since the early days of cinema (the 1913 lost film *The Werewolf* is considered to be the first werewolf movie). Perhaps the most well-known werewolf character is The Wolf Man, first portrayed in Universal Pictures' 1941 movie.

Westlake, Peyton - *See "Darkman"*

Wheelers - Though not featuring in a horror film, the Wheelers, as depicted in the terrifying 1985 children's film *Return to Oz*, are nightmarish characters that utter such child-friendly pleasantries as, "We'll tear you into little pieces and throw you in the deadly desert." Responsible for many cases of childhood trauma.

Wicker statue - A large effigy most commonly used to burn virginial policemen in on remote Hebridean islands - it does help the apple crops, though.

Wilkes, Annie - A fanatical former nurse who rescues her favorite author, Paul Sheldon, from a car crash in the film *Misery* (1990). She forces him to burn the only manuscript of his latest novel; makes him write a new novel featuring her favorite (deceased) character, and smashes both of his feet with a sledgehammer. Not really the best of hosts.

Winchester Tavern - A pub in London that can also be used as a refuge in the event of a zombie apocalypse.

Window - A sheet of glass used to keep the elements out of a building. Quite frequently characters either leap through them or are pushed through them in horror movies.

Wishmaster - *See "Djinn (the)."*

Witch - A wicked, ugly woman with magical, evil powers — traditionally depicted as wearing a pointed hat and flying around on a broomstick. Once upon a time, witches were real, and a rather flawed system of tests was used to determine who was a real witch or not. They pretty much always turned out to be a witch. In horror movies, they tend not to be depicted in their stereotypical manner and can take on many forms.

Witchcraft - The use of magical spells usually, but not always, by witches. It is often associated with black magic, the occult and the devil.

Wolf Creek - A remote attraction in the Australian outback. Wolf Creek National Park is home to a giant crater formed by a massive meteorite and features as a location in the *Wolf Creek* movies. The actual location is the Wolfe Creek Meteorite Crater National Park in Western Australia. Don't accept rides from strangers in the area.

Woodchipper - A machine used to chop up tree limbs or trunks and turn them into woodchips. It can also be used to throw people into.

Woods, The - A common horror film location where cell phones and maps tend to be of no use. Masked killers, ghosts, witches, bears, aliens, monsters and all manner of dreadful things are hiding out there in the woods. Hiding in a cabin won't help you either.

Woodhouse, Rosemary - A New York City gal who had the terrible misfortune to give birth to the Devil's child. Called Adrian.

Worms - A wriggly, slimy-looking limbless creature that's totally harmless but can often be found dangling off the side of a zombie's face, or slithering over a corpse. The 1976 movie *Squirm* chose to feature them more prominently when a violent storm knocked over some power lines and caused the worms to go completely insane! I don't think it was based upon a true story.

X

X rated - A type of film certification often reserved for horror films.

Xenomorph - An alien lifeform hellbent on either killing everyone or cocooning humans to create more alien lifeforms hellbent on either killing everyone or cocooning humans to create more alien lifeforms… etc. Xenomorphs are sharp-toothed aliens with acid for blood and they mostly come out at night… mostly.

Y

Yamamura, Sadako - The name of the long-haired gal in *The Ring* movies. Sadako is a malevolent ghost who, in life, was murdered and thrown down a well, and now is able to return via a cursed video tape. Whoever views the tape will be killed by Sadako seven days after viewing it.

Yankee Pedlar Inn - An historic hotel in Torrington, Connecticut, USA, featured in the 2011 Ti West movie *The Innkeepers*. West was inspired to write the movie having stayed at the hotel whilst filming his 2009 film *The House of the Devil*. The real hotel is purportedly haunted by various spirits, most notably room 353 – the room in which the hotel's original owner Alice Conley died. Echoing events portrayed in the film, the hotel was closed down in 2015. I don't think it was because of ghosts though.

Yautja - An alternative name for the Predator aliens featured in the *Predator* film franchise.

Ygor - *See "Igor."*

Z

Zelda (Goldman) - The name of Rachel Creed's terminally ill, bed-ridden and seriously creepy older sister from *Pet Sematary*. Rachel feels responsible for her death which has led her to become a more monstrous character in her head. Zelda enjoys taunting her younger sister with such playful dialogue as, "I'm going to twist your back like mine, so you'll never get out of bed again." Big sisters can be so mean.

Zodiac Killer - The pseudonym used by the mysterious American serial killer who wrote cryptic letters to the press, taunting them about his crimes, identity and future sadistic plans. He is confirmed as killing five people and remains uncaptured to this day (he's probably dead, though). The Zodiac Killer has made a few horror film appearances over the years (most notably in David Fincher's 2007 non-horror movie, *Zodiac*) in titles such as *The Zodiac* (2005), *Curse of the Zodiac* (2007) and *Awakening the Zodiac* (2017).

Zombie - One of the horror genres most popular types of monster. A zombie is a reanimated corpse, usually devoid of the personality that it had in life, that feeds on the flesh of the living in order to carry on being undead. There are varying reasons for zombies coming back to "life," though sometimes a reason is not specifically alluded to. It is generally accepted that destroying a zombie's brain ("Shoot it in the head!") is the only surefire way to kill a zombie. Depending on which zombie movie you're watching, zombies are either very slow moving or surprisingly fast. Mostly they no longer talk (as they're portrayed as being stupid), they show signs of extreme decay (unless they've only recently been reanimated), they're very resilient to physical attack (but they can't regenerate) and they work very well as part of a team. Zombie outbreaks can occur within a smaller, specified location but quite often their appearance heralds the beginning of a "zombie apocalypse," in which the entire world's population is threatened to be overrun by them.

Zombie movie - A subgenre of horror film featuring zombies. George A Romero's seminal 1968 film, *Night of the Living Dead*, is often regarded as the first modern zombie film that set out many of the rules of the subgenre that are still used in zombie films to this day.

Zuni fetish doll - A freaky doll that is host to an African demon. Zuni is an incredibly angry demon and is also known as, "He Who Kills." He features in the 1975 anthology horror movie, *Trilogy of Terror*.

Zuul - The name of the monstrous Gatekeeper of Gozer in *Ghostbusters*. If you were looking for Dana, I'm afraid you'll only find Zuul.

<u>**A Note From The Author**</u>

Well, first-off, I hope you've enjoyed reading through the entries in this book and I hope you've learnt a thing or two, or at least had a bit of a laugh. When I set out to write this book, I initially thought it wouldn't be such a monumental task. How very wrong I was. The more I researched, the more entries I seemed to uncover. There's plenty that have probably been left out, as I did try to focus on the more popular horror films, as well as some of my personal favorites. It was intended more for the entertainment of my fellow horror fans. Hopefully you'll agree that I haven't done such a bad job of it?

However, if you believe I've made any glaring omissions, or if you have an interesting and more obscure references that you'd like to see included, please feel free to drop me a line and I'll consider adding them for a possible second edition of the book (with a special thanks, of course).

So, a HUGE HORROR THANKS to you for choosing to read this book. Once again, I sincerely hope you enjoyed it. If you did, I would really appreciate a lovely review on Amazon. If you didn't, well, perhaps just keep that to yourself, okay?

Now, onwards with my story, *The Demon of Heritage*, in its full, uncut form!

My very best wishes as always,

Killian
February, 2020, Warrington, England

THE
DEMON OF HERITAGE

(Uncut Version)
By Killian H. Gore

They never really made a good film version of the Bible, but it is where all horror films come from. You got the Apocalypse, you got the Devil, you got zombies with Jesus rising from the dead, you got vampires with the drinking of blood, crucifixion, cults, boom, it's all in the book. Also Churches are the scariest buildings in the world. They're haunted houses.

Marilyn Manson

Your enemy the Devil prowls around like a roaring lion looking for someone to devour.

The New Testament, 1 Peter 5:8,9.

Foreword by Killian H. Gore

The book you are about to read is a reproduction of a diary regarding the previously unreported story of the discovery of a gravestone encountered in the Amazon jungle in 1895 and the subsequent macabre incidents in a small English village that preceded it. Not only have no details been in any way officially documented before but no information could be found anywhere about the existence of the village named in the diary, that of Heritage.

I discovered this journal in a carved wooden box that I found in a walled underground vault unearthed in my garden whilst digging last year. The discovery of the vault was exciting enough, but nothing could quite prepare me for what I found in that box. Initially I speculated that the village I lived in could once have been called Heritage and that the vault belonged to a demolished church. The more I looked into this, the more unlikely it seemed, but not entirely impossible, I suppose.

It is more likely that the box was removed from the village of Heritage and walled up and buried far, far away from its origins, maybe in the hope that it would always remain documented, but never discovered. Or perhaps in the hope that someday the story would be found. I don't know why, or quite how, but I was the one who unearthed this short but astonishing chronicle.

I'm not going to say anything else by way of speculation, I would simply like to reprint this extraordinary diary in its entirety. For the record, the church in which the diary was written is All Hallows Church in Heritage and the year is 1897. The journal begins on the 4th of October and almost entirely focuses upon the story of a gargoyle, a grave and the subsequent horrors conjured by these two seemingly commonplace things. This had led me to believe that this was not the reverend's official journal but more of a diary kept specifically to chronicle the strange chain of events that took place from October to December of that year.

Monday 4th October (1897)

A rather odd thing happened today. A new gargoyle arrived; a most grotesque thing! I had not made any requests for new church decorations, but I suppose some kind soul must have spent some hearty time chiseling away at this ugly statue. Strange that no note was left, just the gargoyle in a rather nice ornate wooden box. Upon regarding further, I looked to the base of the beast (a rather wonderful turn of phrase, I must say!) and observed the word *Kergozu*. I have no concept of what the word means at this present time. I don't believe anyone in the village would have such a queer surname. Perhaps someone not local - from the city, maybe. I'm sure they must have intended to leave a letter of explanation but possibly lost it on route, or it blew away in a freak gust of wind. I trust that whoever the gift bearer was that they will make themselves known during the coming week, failing that in Church this coming Sunday.

Tuesday 5th October

The gargoyle goes up! Braving the dizzying heights, I took Kergozu up onto the ledge at the back of the church. I have decided that the name rather suits him, but I don't know why. Initially I thought I might have needed some expert help in attaching the statue to the building but upon having a short stroll around the grounds I observed the perfect abode. It was a small walled area in which I could simply lodge the gargoyle without the need for any bonding with the surface. It sounds a little strange to say but it was an absolutely perfect fit. Almost as if someone had measured the space and made a sculpture with the correct dimensions. I suppose it's entirely plausible that this was indeed the case. Strange, but possible.

As evil as the little beast looks up there, I wholeheartedly believe it will serve its purpose most wonderfully. Keeping evil away from the church and parishioners. It truly is one of the most chilling gargoyles I have ever observed. It's quite the blood curdling demon! And I'm quite glad he's up there on my church, scaring away even the foulest of evils!

Wednesday 6th October

As I was tending to the gardens, amidst the tombstones today, I glanced up at the church and for a moment I noticed that Kergozu had vanished. A sharp and sudden pain in my head, behind my eyes, urged me to close them and look down momentarily. When I returned my gaze back upon the church, I saw the gargoyle firmly back in place where I had housed him only yesterday. It's funny how the mind can play tricks! Whether it was a trick of the light or just my mind reverting to the more common image of the ledge as it was before the statue's arrival, I do not know.

<u>Thursday 7th October</u>

I found myself back up the ladders again today at the far end of the church, unsure as to quite why I had climbed them. I speculated that it was related to the moment yesterday in which I briefly imagined the gargoyle's disappearance. I think I could have been checking if it indeed was securely in place. I gave it a slight push and pull from side to side, but it didn't move – not one jot! I rocked it a little harder and was surprised to see no movement at all from the stubborn ornament. I decided to attempt to lift Kergozu but for whatever reason I could not elevate the figure from its lodgings. Only yesterday I had not only managed to carry the heavy and cumbersome statue all the way up the ladders but had also carefully slotted it into place on the ledge. I think there may have been some rain during the night, but I can't be sure. If indeed there was then maybe the water had bonded the rock to the church building to some extent. I don't know the science of it all – I'm a man of God, after all!

I found myself walking around the grounds of the church for quite some time during the remainder of the day, despite knowing that I still had some work to do for the Sunday morning worship. It was a little out of character for me to simply wander around, but I felt that the fresh air was good for me and would inspire my forthcoming service in a positive way. It feels as though I have spent the entire day outside. Walking between the gravestones, looking at the many names of the dear departed. I can't truly be sure of all my actions. I must say that I felt slightly in a daze! I'm sure it was a symptom of my contemplating the wondrous place in which all the souls around me were currently residing.

I gave many glances up to the heavens above and it was most joyous to revel in the crisp and cool day as the glaring blue skies dazzled me with their brilliance. Everything was alive and vivid. The heavenly light of the vast cavern overhead was always a dazzlingly beautiful sight to behold. Yet it felt marred at times whenever my gaze fell upon the church. It's difficult to describe but the simplest analogy would be that the sky above was a warm smile, and the church below… well, somehow was more of a frown. A smile it may have nevertheless radiated, but a twisted smile. Dare I say mischievous… malevolent… I do not know. All I can declare is that it unnerved me and gave me a dark feeling inside that I am unaccustomed to especially on the grounds of my own parish where I am normally shrouded in a warm, heavenly glow.

Friday 8th October

I kept seeing things out of place. Not only is this most strange, it is also terribly bothersome. I'm having trouble finding my possessions all of a sudden! When I eased myself from my warm bed this morning, I expected to slide my feet into the sanctuary of my comfortable and fluffy slippers, as I do each and every morning. Instead I had no choice but to place my feet down onto the cold stone floor. My first thought was to check under the bed, speculating that I had accidently pushed them under some time during the night. But the space was void. Dark and empty.

With chilled toes I stepped gently around my immediate surroundings, but to no avail. I should say, to anyone who may read these words someday, that I am not a man accustomed to disorder. Maybe you have already gleaned this from my writings. I would never have left my slippers anywhere other than by the side of my bed. For one thing, I always wear my slippers during the evening and naturally leave them by my bedside before I retire. It would be rather inconceivable of me to leave them elsewhere!

I looked all over my bedroom but simply could not find them. I assumed some type of madness must have taken over me during the previous evening and decided it was time to pray to Saint Anthony. No one could have possibly entered the church during the night so I only had myself to blame. I would like to share the prayer for my journal.

St. Anthony, perfect imitator of Jesus, who received from God the special power of restoring lost things, grant that I may find my slippers that have been lost.

At least restore to me peace and tranquility of mind, the loss of which has afflicted me even more than my material loss. To this favor, I ask another of you: that I may always remain in possession of the true good that is God. Let me rather lose all things than lose God, my supreme good. Let me never suffer the loss of my greatest treasure, eternal life with God.

Amen.

St. Anthony provided for me today for I indeed found my slippers! I have no idea how they arrived at the place they eventually emerged, but I found them. They were outside, on the grounds of the churchyard. I am not accustomed to sleepwalking, but I must have taken a little walk during my rest last night. I believe I must have left my bed and wandered out into the chilled night air to find some comfort. The best explanation I can conjure is that a slight fever overcame me as I slept. The heat of an unsettled stomach or aching head must have driven me from my clammy slumbering state into the salvation of a foreign clime glazed in the sweet icing of a delicious medicine.

I stepped out from the church into the graveyard, repeating the prayer to St. Anthony over and over and I felt drawn to the huge, foreboding silver birch trees at the far end of the grounds. There were fewer tombstones in that particular area as they were for the newer burials. The morning was bright and clean and everything around was radiant, but it could have been the harsh breeze attacking the fading colors of rustling trees that drew me over to the sparse burial space.

As the older headstones subsided from my view, I could clearly observe a pair of slippers amidst the fresher graves. I picked up the cold and slightly dampened shoes and retired back to the church feeling both relived but baffled by the entire episode. When I walked back into my room, I was alarmed to see that the fire was already blazing. Maybe I can be a tad forgetful at times, but I am adamant that I had not ignited a fire that morning. I'm almost a hundred percent sure of this on account of the distraction that the missing slippers provided. I suppose some things that one does by way of routine can often slip from the mind as easily as forgetting each and every breath one takes.

I awoke this morning with a name on my mind. Having gotten myself washed and dressed and fed with a light breakfast of bread and fruit I sat down at my desk and proceeded to study the bible for Sunday's sermon. But the name... *what name?* My thoughts were clearly elsewhere. I began turning the pages of my precious Holy Book endeavoring to find names... or a name within the sweet-scented leaves. Naturally many names presented themselves to me – Daniel, Ezekiel, Samuel, Joshua. It was becoming far too distracting. Names, names, names but none the name on my mind. I wanted nothing more than to pursue my work, but I was becoming increasingly unable to do so. Mentally I felt incapacitated. An illness I was not privy to was attempting to acquaint itself with me.

I thought it best to walk away from my desk and approach the altar for a moment of peace and reflection and prayer – to ask the Lord to calm my thoughts and allow me to focus upon my work – His work, to be pedantic. I knelt down and looked up to the small but vibrant stained-glass window and was just about to close my eyes, clasping my cold hands together, when I observed a chilling and disturbing sight. The altar in my church is adorned with a gold-plated crucifix. It has a sturdy rounded base, rather like a candlestick and is indeed situated between two such candles. I describe it here to illustrate that it is a very heavy object with a substantial base and not the type of ornament that could easily be turned upside down and remain upright.

Yet that is exactly how the crucifix appeared to me.

The robust metal base was now at the top of the cross and the small square area that was the crucifix's head was pressed against the altar. In that first moment of seeing the peculiar sight I briefly speculated if it was indeed possible for such an object to somehow balance in that rather unnatural manner. But my ponderings were abruptly interrupted when the cross toppled over and noisily slammed down onto the awaiting altar. The reverberating, piercing sound was enough to make me doubt what I had witnessed. It gave off such a dramatic pang of noise that it muddied my subsequent thoughts. Even as I write this, I feel deceitful in describing the inverted cross. Maybe I saw it, maybe I didn't. I hope that I did not. In fact, I'm sure I didn't. It would be folly to believe I saw such an unholy thing. *Folly!*

It could be due to the distractions of the previous days, but it is only today that I realized I haven't seen anyone all week – not another living soul! I should state that my church is a mere short stroll away from the first of the houses in Heritage, no more than five minutes at a brisk pace. My own home used to be amongst them but sadly burnt to the ground three years back. I have gotten used to living in the rooms at the far end of the church. There is plenty of space and I am more than happy to live, sleep and wake up in such a harmonious and spiritual environment. Although, that warmness has been marred of late. I would usually see people. I would usually talk with them. People used to visit myself or the church quite frequently. Where is everyone I do wonder?

I decided to have a wander on the grounds of the church to see if I could see anyone in the surrounding area. But all I could see was Kergozu. Each time my head swiveled around I felt drawn to look up at the gargoyle and whenever I did, I felt a stronger vision of the name that had occupied my thoughts recently. For the first time a word appeared to me more clearly – Whitby. I didn't know what it meant but once it entered my mind, I realized it had some association with finding my slippers in the graveyard yesterday morning.

Once again, I felt drawn to the newer graves below the rustling silver birch trees. As I drew closer, I could observe the name Whitby on the freshest tombstone. The blackened letters darkened by shadow radiated a familiar glow. It was the grave that was last in the line – the latest one. Whitby, Thomas Whitby. Trancelike, I glided to the freshly carved granite. Seeing the name filled me with a sense of relief. Indeed, it was the name that had been swilling around my head of late. I can't effectively explain how or why I knew that to be true. It is similar to knowing the answer to a question someone has posed. One's mind goes rather blank with regards the answer. You know what it is; it's something that you have heard and said countless times before but when put on the spot a cloud spoils the view. The uninvited fog drifts over the once clear revelation.

Thomas Whitby. There it was, as clear as Christ. Letters that blazed at me! Thomas Whitby. I muttered the name to myself and commented upon the extraordinary nature of the chain of events that had led me to Mr. Whitby's final resting place. But things were to take a more sinister and confusing turn when I looked down at the words below his name. Firstly, his date of birth – that was nothing unusual, then his date of death. It was Monday the 4th of October 1897. I could feel a wave of dread infest my body and head as I looked at the date. A flash of sickness and maddening head pain that urged me to lose my balance.

In spite of the sudden rush of ill fever I remained upright and focused. There was surely no way that Thomas Whitby, or indeed anyone else, could have been buried at the church upon that date. *It didn't happen!* I could dwell more upon the fact that it didn't happen, but I feel I need to say no more than no one had been buried at the church on Monday the 4th of October 1887. Indeed, there hadn't been a funeral at the church for over a year! The last had been Louis Hart – a very nice elderly gentlemen from the village. Naturally this illustrates the other fact that I know of all the villagers in Heritage. I have lived here for over thirty years and I have never once encountered a gentleman by the name of Thomas Whitby.

I couldn't take my eyes away from the grave for quite some time. Where on earth had it come from? It just wasn't possible. Every theory that raced through my exhausted mind was completely insufficient. No rational reason could be forged to explain what I was being presented with. Minutes may have become hours. I have no idea how long I stood outside with the mystery man.

The mystery grave.

The mystery.

A strange sound from far away jolted me from my temporary trance. It was more the echo from whatever sudden and sharp noise I heard that brought me to. At first, I wasn't too sure what it was but after no more than a couple of seconds it occurred again. I was almost sure it was a scream of some kind. Maybe the cry of a baby. Maybe a lady crying, or shrieking. Maybe the call of an animal. Perhaps a wolf or a cat's high-pitched wailing. Whatever it was it gave me a small fright. I looked down once again at the tombstone just to be sure I hadn't daydreamed the enigma, but Thomas Whitby's October 4th grave was still lying dreadfully at my feet.

I headed back to the church and rushed over to the altar wanting nothing more than to pray long and hard to the good Lord. In fact, I wanted so desperately at that moment to become lost in prayer, to be away from the strange sights and sounds and sensations that were becoming rather too enveloping. But I wasn't to make it to the altar because I could see a dancing, flickering light outside; illuminating the already brilliant colors of the stained-glass window. There were clouds of smoke, heavy and fast, heading for the heavens, and flames, large and wild below them. The sweet smell of burning wood invading my senses. There was a fire raging outside! In the graveyard!

I turned sharply and darted outside through the heavy wooden doors and pelted to the back of the church, expecting to be met by a waft of blinding smoke and all the fires of Hell. But no! No such sight awaited me. Just the green grass, just the chill of the October wind, just the same exterior sights and sounds I had witnessed mere seconds ago, yet I had been so sure I had seen flames bouncing crazily outside the colored glass. I had smelt the smoke and heard the crackle and... it was madness to ruminate on it. Surely it was nothing more than a trick of the light. It was best not to dwell upon it any further, I surmised.

I knelt at the altar and I prayed. I prayed to God for Him to help me make sense of what I was experiencing of late and I remained there until darkness fell. Aside from the incident with the vision of fire through the church window I felt much better to be indoors. I felt protected, but I wasn't quite sure from what. The name of Thomas Whitby was still very much in my thoughts. The more I meditated upon him the more I felt I was visualizing his coffin in my mind. When I closed my eyes, it was there. Dark earth covering up a secret. The box was a light, shining in the gloom...

Sunday 10th October

No one came to church today. Somehow that didn't feel all that peculiar to me. In a way I almost expected it. It was a natural progression of the preceding chain of events. I had awoken early, which was nothing out of the ordinary, but this morning I had awoken with memories of a faraway place – a wild place. In my dream I believe I found it inside Thomas Whitby's grave. There was a jungle down there. A tunnel that led to a brilliant and vibrant celebration of God's creations. Exotic greens of large crisp leaves and glowing reds of incredible flowers that sprouted elegantly from within. It was a veritable garden of Eden indeed! And it was all down there in that dark tomb.

I wasn't sure of the connection. Partly my dreams had shown me these wonders and partly I felt physically compelled to dig up the grave. I didn't really want to go outside again but my thoughts were clouded with whatever was buried at the far end of the graveyard. It never occurred to me that it could be anything bad, more that it would be something that would solve the mysteries that had been occurring all week. Why was I seeing jungles in my head? I couldn't really explain it.

I heard more distant screams as I obtained the spade from the wooden shed around the side of the church. It was not yet the time for the worshippers to begin arriving so I mused, at that moment at least, that I would be undisturbed whilst I was digging. It was around this time that I thought I saw something moving in the grass on the short walk to the far end of the graveyard. The sunlight wasn't quite at its fullest, so it was difficult to distinguish, but it was rather like a shadow that drifted autonomously from physical partner, gliding quickly and smoothly amongst the blades of dew dampened grass. I stepped back, losing my footing, stabbing the spade into the ground and lost sight of the fleeing anomaly. Once I had regained my stance, I looked around for the peculiar shadow but could see nothing more of it.

I continued to my intended destination and after a quick glimpse around for passers-by I drove the spade into the dampened earth and began digging. It was not quite as easy a task as I had thought it would be. Obviously, this was not a job I was accustomed to. All the graves in my churchyard were dug by a man called Kenneth Shaw, but I could hardly call upon him for such an unusual task – he surely wasn't in the habit of digging up graves that had already been dug once before! This really was only something I could do myself despite being unaccustomed to such hard labor.

After making a good start on the arduous task of grave digging (anti-grave digging) I lay down a black sheet on top of the hole and threw some dirt over it. It had quickly become time for Sunday morning worship. I had nothing prepared, but I felt I would have plenty of stories to tell the congregation. I stood by the church doors, having opened them in preparation for the flock, and waited. The view from the church entrance allows me to see up the road that approaches the church and I would normally at this time see the villagers, all bright and beautiful, gaily making their way over to be greeted by me. But the road this morning was empty.

I did contemplate making the short trip into the village, but I felt afraid. Besides, I had work to do! There was a mystery to be solved and Thomas Whitby had all the answers. I closed the church doors and headed back for some more hard work. As I walked, I saw the strange shape in the grass once more, but this time I was able to determine what it was. It was a creature that I had only seen before in books. It was a snake! I realize that there are wild snakes in England, but I was quite startled to see one out in the open. Sadly, there was no time to observe it in any detail as it vanished from my sight with incredible speed. I only wish I had that kind of energy!

The digging continued for what felt like most of the day, but it proved rather fruitless. I cannot say for sure how deep I dug but I knew I could not go on any further. The above skies were grey with foreboding patches of black cloud drifting here and there. I walked back to the church in need of some nourishment and a nice hot cup of tea to revive myself. My night was to be a short one. I took to my bed and pulled the covers over my head.

<u>Monday 11th October</u>

More dreams flooded my mind during the previous night's sleep. One image that gave me a chill was a black snake slowly slithering over the Kergozu gargoyle outside the church. A snake that had eyes that glowed a devilish red. The light blazed from within them and coated the statue with traces of red… a red that became liquid… that became blood. Blood that oozed from both the snake and the statue and began to drip down the sides of the church. The blood was everywhere! More and more snakes began to coat the church until the entire building moved and writhed like a colossal living organism. The blood flooded the churchyard transforming it into a lake that surrounded the building, making an island of it.

Large trees floated throughout this blood-lake, but not trees that belonged in the English countryside. These were trees from faraway lands. Big trees that one would find in a jungle deep in the Amazon rainforest. They floated by in increasing numbers and it became apparent that this was not a lake but a huge river of blood. Everything was propelling forward at a terrific speed. Amidst the jungle trees the snake-infested church bobbed and rocked in the chaotic crimson river. The whole ensemble headed for an immense waterfall. Trees dropped out of sight as the blood rushed over the blackened edge. The sound of the falls became a deafening roar and the rage of both sound and vision increased as the church drew closer to its ultimate demise.

Faces of my helpless friends, my congregation, the villagers, my parents… all the visages of everyone I had ever known and loved, were gathered at the grotesque stained-glass windows; their bloodied hands scratching deep and visible marks into the indestructible panes. I could observe the horror in the eyes of each and every living soul held captive inside – knowing eyes that performed the tragedy of the violent demise they were to defenselessly endure.

The fires of hell awaited those imprisoned inside as the infested chapel dropped from the bloodied water's edge and plunged into the demonic inferno. I heard screaming as it descended. I heard nothing *but* screaming. The jungle resonances and once deafening roar of the blood-waterfall subsided entirely. There were only the screams. Men, women and children. Every living soul inside the church. All crying out in pain as the raging fires engulfed them. The screaming became more and more infused with waking life until I realized I was lying in my bed. I continued to hear the screaming for a moment or two as I lay there in stark reality. It was far more distant than in the dream and I wondered if I had indeed heard it for real or merely as an echo from my recent nightmare.

Once I believed myself truly awake and free from dreaming, I stepped out of bed and was surprised to feel that the floor was warm. Not even during the summer would I ever feel a rise in temperature on the cold grey slabs. As I walked around the church the sensation of heat was everywhere. There was sweat upon my forehead despite having not yet begun the completion of yesterday's exerting task. But that was the first port of call for the day, after dressing and having a small breakfast of biscuits and tea.

The humidity continued outside. It was unnaturally warm, and I found myself dripping with sweat before I had even started digging at the ground. I knew it wouldn't take me too long today to reach the buried box that (surely) would hold the answers to at least some of the mysteries. So, I started the task with an eagerness fueled by the hopefully imminent conclusion to the tale that had written itself around me over the past days.

Only perhaps an hour had passed when my spade thudded down on the coffin lid. In that time, I had seen two or three more snakes around the churchyard. I presumed there to be a nest in the surrounding woods (if, indeed snakes have nests – it's not really a subject I have any authority on). I continued to lift the soil off with the spade until most of the lid was exposed. I pulled myself out of the tomb and looked down at the grubby coffin. I felt both disappointed and exhilarated simultaneously. Disappointed to have merely unearthed a coffin instead of something more unusual but exhilarated by seeing just who the mysterious Thomas Whitby was.

I headed back to the toolshed to find an axe to smash the coffin open with. I had considered prizing it open more carefully but a sense of urgency had clearly pervaded my thinking of late. It wasn't as if I was endangering the life of anyone in the box, after all! As I strode back, I must have seen two or three more snakes – one of them swooshed directly in front of me. It was a long and thick creature, colored red and black. Very exotic looking and not something I believe I have ever known to be an English snake but, as I've stated before, I'm no expert on such matters.

I returned to the grave and placed the axe on the grass before carefully sliding down into the gloomy hole. I composed myself for a short moment, looking up to the bright blue sky and wiping the flowing sweat from my brow, before reaching for the axe and holding it above my head. The craziness of what I was doing somehow eluded me as I dropped the heavy tool down onto the mystery dead man's final resting place – were these the actions of a man of God?

I dropped the axe down in the middle of the coffin to provide myself a gap to pull away the wood and glimpse at the interior. After the first strike my work was temporarily halted when I heard a growl from the graveyard above me. It's difficult to describe it in any further detail, for I have no real frame of reference for such a sound. A year or so back I was lucky enough to visit a new zoo that had opened in the city some forty miles west of Heritage. There were plenty of wild animal sounds to be heard during that excursion, but I wouldn't really know one growl from another. But I knew when I heard it that it was not the sound of an animal indigenous to England.

And this thought terrified me.

The snakes could be explained, or so I thought at the time, but this growl was definitely a beast from distant lands. No cat or dog, cow or horse from the English isles was capable of such a guttural, malevolent growl. I deliberated through all the plausible animals that I could conjure from memory that could offer some glimpse of explanation. Partly I did this to distract myself from the horror above me and partly to rationalize the sound. The weight of the axe then began to outweigh the musings of my mind and I realized I was armed with a very effective weapon to defend myself from whatever was stalking the once peaceful church grounds.

I lifted the axe up above the edges of the open grave, hoping to show the growling beast that I was not one to be trifled with. The heavy blade, glinting in the bright sunlight, arose from the tomb closely but timidly followed by the tip of my head. Axe and man peered out into the wild; uncertain of what exactly was about to meet their gaze. Had the axe not been such a weighty object I'm sure it would have quivered with my fear, allowing the awaiting creature to note my comparative weakness and lurch for me, making a quick meal of its physically inferior prey.

I raised myself higher, and as my immediate view of jagged blades of grass subsided, I was able to observe the more complete vista of the churchyard. A quick perusal of the surroundings showed nothing out of the ordinary. No wild animals… no animals at all! Just everything as it had been before I had dug myself six feet under.

I looked from left to right and for the slightest moment thought I saw something moving in the bushes but dismissed it rather quickly as nothing more than the breeze.

I turned back to the coffin and without hesitation dropped it down for a second time onto the soiled wooden box, causing sharp splinters of wood to jolt up like a predator's claws at me. It only took a few more swings before the resulting hole was large enough to gape inside the darkened box. I have seen plenty of dead bodies before so I wasn't too apprehensive at observing the corpse of Thomas Whitby, however, the expected macabre contents were not what greeted me.

There were no human remains to be uncovered from within; only a collection of papers.

I lifted myself out from the grave and eagerly strolled back to the church. Again, I was aware of anomalous sounds haunting my senses, but I was far too determined to return indoors to be halted by them. I write this having just returned inside. I am feeling unnaturally hot and somewhat feverish. I cannot be sure at this present time if it's merely a result of my strenuous work or the clammy weather. I intend to go to my bed and begin looking through the mysterious papers. Hopefully the revelations within will reignite my current lapse of energy.

Saturday 16th October

I have scarcely left my bed since earlier in the week. A fever overtook me more completely than I had initially believed it would. Thankfully I had just enough supplies within the church that could sustain me for such a length of time. Not that I have felt all that willing to partake in a hearty diet. The heat has been terrible for this time of year. A blazing blue sky has sparkled through from beyond my heavy black curtains, giving them the appearance of a beautifully brilliant night sky. And yet I have also been aware of countless storms peppering the unseasonal climate. Thunder and lightning has rumbled and flashed, and rain has pelted the church with a vengeance.

Even stranger, with all the days that have passed since digging up Thomas Whitby's grave, I have not had one visitor to the church. I have decided that on the morrow I will venture into the village. Aside from inquiring why they have not visited recently I will also need to stock up on my diminishing supplies. I can only speculate at this point but perhaps the same fever that has recently had its cold, sweating hands around my health for this past week had its origins in the village. Maybe they have all found themselves resigned to their beds too.

I wonder if like myself they took to reading whilst overcoming their incapacitating symptoms? I doubt that they would have had the same caliber of incredible manuscript that I distracted myself with. Thomas Whitby's handwritten accounts of his journey into the Amazon jungle had taken me into another world. I felt as though I were there with him on his adventure, and as I drifted in and out of consciousness and my ill health doped my sense of reality I indeed felt as though I was deep in the jungle with Thomas.

Quite possibly his story is one of the strangest pieces of work I have ever read, and I am unsure at this time how much I believe to be true. It is entirely plausible that Mr. Whitby was merely a very imaginative writer. In my present state of mind, having just emerged from a feverish delirium, I am rather more susceptible to such absurd and ungodly speculations. The recent chain of events at the church have unsettled my usually stable mind and muddled my opinion on what to believe true and what false - or imagined, indeed.

I am keen to head into the village as I write this, despite wanting to chronicle the more bizarre information gleaned from Thomas' diaries. I am craving some decent sustenance; my body having been weakened by days of substandard consumption. I want some fresh bread! My basic human need for food is dizzying my rationale. Perhaps after regaining my strength with some solid and fresh village delights, I can begin to rethink, reevaluate and rationalize Thomas Whitby's strange story. It's rather amazing and almost humorous that my thoughts have turned to something as base as food having just absorbed such a tale that has shook and disturbed and frightened me so! Though at this time, it is a story without ending. I believe that buried down in the recently unearthed coffin are more pages, more answers and hopefully some linkage between what happened out there in the wild and untamed jungles of the Amazon and my quaint little church in the pleasant countryside of my dearest England.

<u>Sunday 17th October (Morning)</u>

I have just been into the village. I haven't brought back any supplies. My time there was very, very brief. My hands are still shaking from what I observed. I have tried to calm myself with a little brandy, enough to at least allow myself to attempt a short chronicle of the horror I witnessed. *Dear God! Oh, Dear God!* What has happened here in Heritage?

They are all dead. Every last one of them. Men, woman and… dear Lord no… all the children. *Dead, all of them!* The bodies were everywhere. The blood… at first sight I thought reddened autumnal leaves adorned the village square. But, no, 'twas blood! The blood that had flowed from the village's entire population painted the roads, painted the walls of the houses - painted everything and everywhere and everyone.

I saw mutilated bodies. I saw flesh and bone, everything coated in a black mist that I soon realized was ravenous insects feasting on the grotesque meat of the fallen. In mere minutes I saw more blood, gore, death and decay than my eyes could sustain and soon the tears blinded me and for blissful seconds I saw nothing.

During the nothing I turned and stumbled away from the carnage and staggered back down the lane away from the village, my return journey fraught with chaos. Frequently falling, my eyes never able to readjust themselves back to the twisted new reality I was caught up in. I incurred injury after injury as I crawled, walked, ran and floated back to my church.

As I traversed the road my initial emotion was pure fear – a fear that drove me to escape the horror as quickly as I possibly could. I barely had any free thought to allow me to rationalize what I had seen. I was only focused on leaving behind the hellish version of the once tranquil village square I had so often frequented in the past - a past that now seemed more like weeks, months, even years away. Regardless of my familiar surroundings I felt totally lost. My once familiar landscape was now a foreign land to me.

I don't know what to do. I can't think what else to write. I need some time to contemplate, reflect, pray and only then attempt to somehow relax and calm myself down. Everything is still far too hazy.

Sunday 17th October (Afternoon)

I have decided that I must venture back into the village. Although it is unlikely, there could be survivors of whatever horror has swept over Heritage's residents. All I can hope is that the perpetrator (be it a person, or group, or animal or… something else) has long since relinquished. I write this now by way of explaining to whomever may one day find this why there may be no more entries, in case the evildoer or evildoers are still a tangible threat. May God protect me. I have my Bible with me, and the Lord shall walk with me.

Sunday 17th October (Evening)

No one was alive. I saw the dead bodies of the friends that I knew and loved this afternoon. I saw their violently mutilated bodies. I saw horrors I never believed I would ever have to encounter outside of my nightmares. I checked every house, every shop, every place of business. The dead were everywhere. Some of them I could not determine the exact nature of their death. Others I could easily observe had been stabbed. In some cases, I saw large pegs or hooks embedded into people's foreheads. Some of them had been cut into pieces. Whenever I thought I saw movement it was worms or maggots or flies feeding upon the villagers remains. Rats, spiders and… perhaps I also saw snakes.

I spoke as best I could from the Bible wherever I went. I spoke aloud as I walked. At times my voice was raised to the level of shouting, a torrent of divine verse hurled at the Devil's work. I damn near screamed! As I think about it this evening, I suppose that it is entirely possible that my hysterical delivery of God's heavenly words were not only to heighten their impact on the dreadful scenes around me but to dampen something out. For every now and then, and at first it seemed only distant, I was sure I heard laughter. Not the playful, humorous laughter of friends enjoying themselves but the laughter of someone with a twisted mind laughing at another's misfortune. An evil laugh that, had I not raised my voice so loud, would have driven me insane with its sheer, foreboding malevolence.

All around me I felt its sneer. It was as if the blood and gore mocked me. Every now and then it felt like the rotted faces were smirking at me. Where once I spied an expression of horror on the dead, there seemed momentarily a glance of a dark and dreadful smile. Surely it could not have been real? I prayed to God that all I saw were happy smiles of those departed souls who had crossed over and entered the gates of Heaven.

And God shall wipe away all tears from their eyes; and there shall be no more death, neither sorrow, nor crying, neither shall there be any more pain: for the former things are passed away.

Monday 18th October (Morning)

The stench of death is everywhere. I fear that I myself may not have much longer before I am welcomed at the blessed gates of Heaven. My previous night's sleep was once again marred by terrible sights and sounds. I can no longer distinguish the difference between things that I have seen, things which I have read and things that my resting mind has conjured. Everything blends and bleeds into each other.

I saw wild beasts prowling the village streets invading the tranquil homes of the innocent residents. Monstrous crocodiles with gaping jaws of bladelike teeth snapping down on the weak flesh of the terrified elderly and young. Huge snakes wrapping their exotically decorated bodies around men and women, squeezing them with such terrific force that their preys' eyes seeped from their sockets to be pecked and consumed by awaiting vultures.

Terrifying sea beasts emerged from the placid ponds of the once serene parks and woodlands where children played. Bloodied mouths of large, impossibly sharp and heavy teeth, leaping from the blackened waters and crunching down, bursting the bodies of the vulnerable youngsters; blood wildly spraying as the body parts were chaotically jettisoned into the skeletal branches.

I feel that I can't go on. I'm so afraid and dreadfully lonely. I have called upon the Lord, but I fear that He does not listen. How can He have created a world in which such horrors are allowed to prevail? Is this the work of the Devil himself? Has Satan's grip on God's creation taken over? I am doubting my senses. Since I awoke this morning, I have had an overwhelming feeling of being watched. From the walls, from the ceilings, from the eyes in the paintings and through the windows. Someone or something is watching me. Intently.

Thomas Whitby's journal has continued to haunt my thoughts during these horrifying days. In his travels to the Amazon rainforest he had written about being lost deep in the jungle. For fear that his diary will vanish as bizarrely as it arrived in my possession, I transcribe his accounts in verbatim for posterity.

There is not another soul around. I have lost count of how many days I have been alone out here. It feels like weeks. Despite the obvious solitude and lack of food I have felt neither hungry nor lonely. The statue has kept me company and dissipated any need for nourishment. Kergozu looks after me.

As I write this it is the dead of night in the jungle, yet Kergozu emanates a peculiar radiance of light that allows me to write these words. And what words they shall be! Words that no-one is sure to believe nor may ever read. I know now that I should likely die out here. But knowing that does not fill me with a sense of dread at all. I'm not entirely sure how it does make me feel. My thoughts have not quite been my own since becoming lost out here.

To think this all began by my stumbling across the gargoyle deep in the Amazon rainforest. It was not at all what I expected I would discover out here. At first it had frightened me to my very core. My first sight of it, from a distance, had been more like a small black cloud. Flies buzzed around the object that I could not yet make out.

As I neared the fluttering apparition, I could observe a solid shape that it shrouded. Some type of statue. I wafted the flies aside once I was much closer and it took much doing for the vermin to fully dissipate. Once the vast majority had vaguely cleared, I was able to look upon the ugly stone beast with greater ease. I recognized it as the type of carving that one would find adorning the exterior walls of a church. But there was something altogether more unfamiliar about it. It was far more vivid than any I had ever viewed before. Perhaps this was due to my proximity to it.

In spite of myself I turned to see if my guides had followed me. I didn't really desire to turn away from the anomalous object for it had somewhat entranced me — perhaps simply as a result of its anomalous nature. This was the first moment I realized I was alone. It didn't worry me as I knew they would not fully abandon me. Likely they were worried about my discovery and were keeping a safe distance. They were master hunters and could easily blend into their surroundings to catch jungle beasts for food.

As I turned back to the statue I was able to see it in a slightly different manner. Prior to this my focus had been entirely on the monster and not its surroundings. Below it was a rectangle of upturned land. Taking a few steps back it became apparent that I had been stood upon a recently dug grave and that the gargoyle was some type of headstone — but for whom? There was no name anywhere upon it. Stepping off the dampened, muddy earth I ventured nearer to the marker and could observe no engraved words English or otherwise.

I looked back down at the upturned land and surmised that it must have been quite a recent burial. I wanted to ask my companions if they knew anything about its origins, so I turned and called to them but to no avail. Repeatedly I shouted, fearless of announcing my abundance of warm flesh to possible hungry predators in the vicinity, but no reply was retorted, and I considered leaving the burial site and seeking them out, but something I cannot explain compelled me to remain where I was. In some way I felt rooted to the spot.

I can only speculate that something about the small area I found myself in reminded me of home, of England. Despite it not being a typical gravestone by a large margin it was strongly reminiscent of the usual headstone and upturned earth that one has seen on many sad occasions at home. And even though it was a rather grim reminiscence, in this foreign land, in this dense and alien jungle it was worth its weight in gold and warmed me in a way that the heat of the Amazon jungle could not.

I sat myself down adjacent to the grave and headstone and looked up at Kergozu.

Kergozu? Why had I named him so? I had no idea. The name had conjured so speedily into my thoughts as I looked up at him. It made no sense to me and was a name without reference or influence. Had it been a word used by one of the tribesmen that were acting as my guides? It was entirely possible. My grasp on their language was incredibly limited. They spoke so little both to me and amongst themselves that I was almost sure I would have remembered this particular word. Such a stark and memorable word that it was.

I will do my best to describe Kergozu but it is with some difficultly that I attempt to do so as his appearance seemed to alter with every new glance. He had quite a wolf-like appearance with a long snouted nose and gaping mouth that sometimes seemed to have teeth in it and other times not. A large tongue protruded from the mouth which itself was stretched back in an almost smile. But there was something about the attempted smile that wasn't particularly benevolent. I wouldn't go so far as describe it as malevolent either though sometimes as shadows from the jungle canopy waved over his features a certain menace momentarily became prevalent.

Atop his head were two stumps that were much like shorter and thicker versions of those on a goat's head and to the side two triangular ears that showed some signs of damage as if they'd been caught on something. His eyebrows were one of his more startling features. Heavily set in a frown and placed directly above the eyes with no apparent gap that would adorn a human's features. There definitely was something menacing about him but, strangely, something jovial too. He frightened and amused me in equal measure in a way no other work of art had ever stirred me.

I thought as I looked at him that I heard the sound of laughing in the far distance, but I couldn't conceive how this could be so. Were my guides watching me and finding my fascination with this gravesite amusing? Were they privy to something I was unaware of? The laughter seemed to grow in volume and was not of the type I was accustomed to in the music halls of England. It was rather more sinister.

My focus remained on the face of Kergozu. Was it indeed he laughing at me? The sound was drifting from all around and I felt myself wandering into an alternative state, dangerously so, as if under the influence of a powerful hallucinogenic drug. It was so overwhelming that I got to my feet and turned away from him to face the jungle once again. The shock of my sudden momentum dragged me sharply back into the reality I had come accustomed to over the past few months and I came to the realization that the sound was nothing more than the chirping of the numerous exotic birds and other foreign creatures whose domain I currently resided in.

Kergozu's stony eyes glared at me as the laughter diminished, replaced by words that manifested in my mind. I felt the statue urging me to dig the grave up for whatever reason I could not possibly fathom. I had no reason or want to ignore the subconscious request and so I reached for my small trowel which hung from my belt and vehemently began digging. It was quite a sweltering task in the oppressive heat of the jungle but one that I was keenly focused upon achieving for reasons that were not prominent to me.

Finally, I reached a dark box. Of course, everything down in the shaded jungle in a dark hole was naturally dark but there was something unnaturally dark about the box. It was a black darker than any other. So black it initially seemed that nothing at all was actually there. Certainly no physical object. Knocking upon it with the handle of my trowel was the only way to ascertain that it indeed was tangible, but I abstained from such an action for fear of losing the tool or indeed myself, physically or otherwise.

I cleared the dirt from the top end of the black box to discover some kind of written symbols carved into the strange material. My prior scholarly pursuits aided my observation of the word as being one written in Hebrew. The English translation of it would be Abaddon. This I found to be particularly worrisome as the word means destruction or place of destruction. I further fear that it has associations with Satan. My knowledge is not absolute on the subject — what I'd give for a library in this Godforsaken land!

But how peculiar that such a word be uncovered here of all places! I'm deep in the wilderness so far away from the rest of the world. How is it even possible? It's entirely unfathomably that such an item purporting that word could have wended its way to this burial site so deep in the jungle. It's madness! I contemplated that some exotic fever could have overtaken my mind and caused me to incur seeing things that weren't there.

I crept up out of the grave upon realizing that it didn't seem to be a stable surface at all. The words etched upon the blackness had appeared to hover rather than behave more like a physical word written on a physical object. Abaddon glided and quivered like a name written upon water. Black water. So very black, so very endless, so very bleak yet so very entrancing - hypnotic. I felt that if I stared any more, I would fall down into it and never again reemerge.

As I returned to the solid earth of the jungle I was shocked to see that night had fallen around my surroundings. But not so my immediate surroundings, for this is when I first observed the strange light that Kergozu offered. Upon glancing down at my watch, I witnessed the hands racing forwards, hours and hours passing before my very eyes. I looked up to see night turn to day then night again three times over until all fell very still and silent as night once again enveloped. The usual melodies of the jungle subsided, and I found myself sitting side by side with Kergozu like old acquaintances.

He talks to me as I try to accommodate my own thoughts on top of his. Transcribing his words and my own, melding them together to…

I don't know what I'm thinking anymore.

And the great dragon was cast out, that old serpent called the Devil and Satan which deceiveth the whole world: he was cast out into the world, and his angels were cast out with him. And they had a King over them, the angel of the bottomless pit whose name in the Hebrew tongue is Abaddon.

The words seemed to manifest from somewhere else and I began to see all around me fire and snow. Kergozu is looking down at me, his grin both malevolent and jovial as he talks. I see now that he indeed talks! His mouth moves as he describes hellish scenes of which I dare not describe. And he urges me, tells me over and over that I must seek solace in the blackness at our feet. He conveys to me I must hold onto him and take him down into the pit with me. And as I look down into the black pool I uncovered all I want is to slide down into its warm and welcoming eternity with Kergozu at my side.

<u>Monday 18th October (Afternoon)</u>

Having remained locked in my homely quarters all morning rereading

Mr. Whitby's incredible words, the prevailing feeling of being observed led me into the Church's nave. And I was not alone in there. Situated on the left wall is a large statue of Christ on the crucifix. I had been approaching the altar when it caught my eye. At first, I felt as though Jesus' eyes were watching me. I had only sensed the slightest of movements as I glanced over at the life-like flesh colors of the beautifully crafted image of our Lord and savior. Primarily I continued on my path to the altar a few more steps until a much greater movement at my side triggered me to cease walking and sharply turn my head back to the crucifix.

Blood was flowing from Christ's head where the thorns dug into his skull. I saw water in his eyes. It glistened from the bright sunlight that flooded the church interior. The crown of thorns no longer appeared molded and painted - they were fresh; they were real. As real as Jesus's eyes that were now focused unequivocally upon me. Eyes that had once pointed to the heavens were now staring into mine. I felt as nailed to the spot as he was to the cross. Dark red blood continued to gently glide from the wounds on his head streaking his thin and gaunt face.

More blood cascaded from the fresh injuries on his body. The gaping holes that housed the nails in his hands and feet were small waterfalls of thick and dark oozing blood. As the fluids dripped with audible splashes onto the hard stone floor Jesus kept his gaze firmly upon me. At first his expression was solely one of pain. The agony and suffering of his disposition copiously radiated his every feature. Trickles of blood from his twisted nest of needled-thorns that tangled into his hair meandered their way down his forehead and into his eyes. He closed them for a matter of seconds and as he opened them again I found myself screaming in unflinching terror.

His eyes had flicked open as if he had abruptly awoken from a dreadful dream. They were now blood red and malevolent. The expression on his awoken face had been first a crazed and maddening stare, the agony still very much apparent, but as he looked deeply into me his expression changed. My scream followed the haunting conversion of his demeanor. His lips had spread outwards, mutating from thin to thick as a smile grew on his pulped face. It was wide enough to show his gritted and bloodied teeth. His wide eyes bulged from their sockets. There was no happiness to be seen. It was an evil smile. Mischievous and threatening. I could never before have imagined such a horrible face forming on the features of our Lord.

I dropped to the floor and cradled my face with my hands, not wishing to look any longer into the horrifically distorted face of the incarnate demonic Jesus. I wept and uttered words of total gibberish into the only means of escape available to me. But the shield my quivering hands gave wasn't enough to defend from the sounds reverberating around me. At first it was merely the gentle splatter of liquid onto stone floor but in the darkness further sounds emerged. Sounds and words.

I realized I was chanting prayer into my hands. *Lord have mercy, Christ have mercy, Lord have mercy, Christ have mercy.* Over and over. Until more words flooded into my dizzying mind.

We drive you from us, whoever you may be, unclean spirits, all satanic powers, all infernal invaders, all wicked legions, assemblies and sects. In the name and by the power of Our Lord Jesus Christ, may you be snatched away and driven from the Church of God and from the souls made to the image and likeness of God and redeemed by the Precious Blood of the Divine Lamb.

The drip, drip, drip of blood had lessened as I prayed until everything returned to silence. I was beginning to lift my head from my hands when I heard the voice in the blackness of my grasp. A dark, guttural voice that seemingly echoed all around the church, seeping into every nook and cranny. A voice that I felt resonate through me and within me.

"I AM KERGOZU," it said.

<u>Monday 18th October (Evening)</u>

I was awoken by the roar of a wild animal. The voice in the church had startled and shaken me, physically and mentally, to the extent that I had fainted through fear and exhaustion. The near darkness provided by my hands had led to an unconsciousness that enveloped all senses and somehow transported me away from the church to a place that I didn't primarily recognize. At first, I was unsure if the growl had occurred in my sleeping mind. I looked up and observed a familiar image, but one now tainted with an otherworldly red tint. It was the sky as I had rarely observed it, perhaps not ever.

The clouds were heavy and black and as free flowing as smoke from a chimney. Behind them the sky was a starkly ominous cerise. Everything was eerily silent for a few moments before I heard the roar again. This time I was certain I was no longer dreaming. I briefly speculated that it could simply be thunder as the sky appeared dark and stormy. But there were traits in the sound that heavily favored it being generated by a living creature - by some enormous beast.

As my senses gathered into coherence, I realized I was not lay upon the grass outside the church - I was in a hole of some kind. All around me were the dark and muddied walls of a freshly dug pit. It occurred to me that I could only really be in one place: Thomas Whitby's grave. I had no idea if I had slept-walked to the area during my slumber or if I had fled the church and fallen into the hole accidently, injuring my head and rendering myself unconscious.

Underneath me was Mr. Whitby's vandalized coffin, the shards of broken wood digging uncomfortably into my back. But this seemed the least of my worries as I heard once again the animal stalking the church grounds above me. It sounded closer than before, perhaps just sitting and waiting at the foot of the grave. What if it were to peer down and see me in this small ditch? I would have no escape. My only possible refuge would be attempting to break away more of the coffin and clamber inside. But that would be ridiculous and unfeasible. Besides, the animal would have doubtlessly torn me limb from limb before I could attempt such a fruitless flight.

I put my hands onto the surface of the coffin and broke away one of the larger splinters of wood that I had smashed with the axe previously. Defending myself from the awaiting animal seemed a far more plausible option. In all likelihood it wouldn't be much of a fair fight if the animal was anywhere near as ferocious as its growl, but under the circumstances it was all I feared I could do.

Above me all had been reduced to silence and had been for quite some time when I decided to slowly rise from the grave and survey the churchyard. I kept my movements to the bare minimum, easing my head out from the hole as nimbly as a predator stalking its prey (which seemed something of a contradiction, really). Unfortunately, the fragile surface I was standing upon was unable to hold my weight and my foot broke through the crumbling terrain. I fell back onto the coffin, falling through completely as the entire lid collapsed with my weight.

Temporarily I must have lost all my senses for I did not feel any pain nor recall any sights or sounds. A great all-encompassing numbness had cloaked my very being. Under normal circumstances I could have ascertained the duration of my unconsciousness, but I was clueless.

I carefully clambered out of the frightful grave, firstly checking the surrounding area, which appeared devoid of anything potentially threatening. Whatever had been roaming in the graveyard, if indeed anything at all actually had, was now no longer occupying or prowling the grounds. I retired to my bed in a dual state of bewilderment infused with a somehow perfect clarity.

Friday 19th November

A month has passed since my last entry, but I do not know how. After falling through the coffin and retiring to bed I do not recall anything else. I quite simply refuse to believe I lay unconscious in Thomas Whitby's grave for an entire month! That would constitute the ramblings of a mad man! Which, dear Lord, maybe I have become. The only physical evidence that the event actually occurred is the scroll that was in my grasp when I awoke. This was certainly obtained from within the demolished casket belonging to Mr. Whitby.

I have just read through the contents of that scroll. It has filled me with a deep sense of dread. For it contains not the words of Thomas Whitby but the words of Kergozu. I can only speculate that during his time at the mysterious grave in the Amazon jungle Mr. Whitby was somehow instructed by this demon to translate the gargoyle's thoughts into words. It is with some sense of trepidation that I choose to transcribe those words into my own journal.

The fire's do go out for I have seen such a thing on many occasions. We don't burn and burn. Only on Earth do they burn and burn. Madness, mayhem; all that is unholy is all on the earth. We do not burn and burn.

The sea gave up the dead that were in it, and death and Hades gave up the dead that were in them, and each person was judged according to what he had done. Then death and Hades were thrown into the lake of fire. The lake of fire is the second death.

Anger courses through me. Burns stronger than any fire at the teachings of such madmen. No-one knows evil as I do. No-one lives it more than I do. I inhabit the stone. I live and breathe through stone and through fire. Glinting out, peering into other worlds. 'Tis me, the evil face that you see and seek. Everywhere I dwell, I am everywhere. I am eternal. Eternal evil plaguing you at every juncture.

And he opened the bottomless pit; and there arose a smoke out of the pit, as the smoke of a great furnace; and the sun and the air were darkened by reason of the smoke of the pit.

Join me in the pit, join me in hell. Forever feel the warmth and joy of evil

Upon full unraveling of the scroll I also realized I had in my possession a map. It had fallen from the scroll as if lodged in there. I am unsure if it is Thomas Whitby's or Kergozu's work, but it is certainly appears to be a map of the jungle in the Amazon where Thomas discovered the grave.

<u>December – Date unknown</u>

Such beastly horrors! Such unspeakable terror! Upon opening the doors at the front of the church I was greeted by the strangest combination of both fire and snow. It was an impossible spectacle to behold. All around the fire's burned and reflected in the sky as a grim blood red. The once gentle sight of feathery snowflakes turned my face as white as they; fluttering from the dark skies more like ash from a hellish fire, scolding my cheeks with a sapping bite.

The brief moment I stood at the door looking upon the catastrophic imbalance of the world was enough to witness something so otherworldly that I felt I had remained there for an eternity. Time no longer flows in quite the steady linear manner I have always been accustomed.

Great beasts were flying with birdlike precision in the whirling blood-tinged snowflakes. Primarily they appeared to be locusts but were more like horses with long flowing hair and large pointed teeth like those of a lion, when viewed more keenly. Huge wings protruded from their backs as they swarmed their ghastly path through the once tranquil Heritage. I swung the heavy doors of the church firmly shut and darted from the unbelievable chaos on my doorstep.

As I fled to my quarters, I realized with a sudden gasp that I had one parishioner present for an unscheduled sermon. But he was not one of my usual flock - far, far from it. He sat on the front row, perched on a pew looking not forward to the altar but directly at me.

Kergozu and I locked eyes. Despite staring merely into stone there was something alive about those eyes. They were most certainly not human but were the eyes of a living creature, nonetheless. Taking my lesson from the ill-fated words of Thomas Whitby I looked away from Kergozu. I would not allow him into my thoughts nor give him voice. He had said and done enough. Gazing upon him, observing him, acknowledging his existence would only imbue him with the power he clearly so desired.

I averted my eyes and walked past Kergozu into my quarters to chronicle these ungodly events.

Late December

I realize now that I must seek out the gravesite in the Amazon jungle described in the notes. I do not yet know how I will accomplish such an incredible feat, but I must! I quite simply must! The tomb needs to be sealed; the darkness needs to be quashed. I dare not throw Kergozu back into the grave as Thomas did, for I know not where he may emerge next. The open grave has plainly released something into this world that needs to be sealed for as long as I can endure. As for Kergozu's fate, he is mere limestone. He will crumble with time. My trusty axe will help him on his way.

I do not know if I shall survive this undertaking or ever return. It may be my God given duty to forever guard this world from the evil lurking in the dark of that bottomless pit. It may be a futile task. It may not.

God be with me.
Reverend Thomas Whitby, December 1887, Heritage, England.